Books written by C.C. Wills

THE TREASURE TRILOGY:

Treasure in the Shawnee Hills

Shawnee: The Adventure Continues

A Cherokee Wish

Other Books:

Memories

Short Stories:

Bite of the Grizzly

Author's website:

http://www.ccwills-author.com

Member of the **Illinois Authors Wiki** and **Illinois Reads**

MEMORIES

by

C.C. WILLS

C.C. Wills

Grape Creek Publishing

Danville, Illinois

Copyright © 2014 by C.C. Wills
First Edition – April 2014

ISBN
978-0-9857957-0-2 (Paperback)
978-0-9857957-1-9 (Hardback)

All rights reserved.

Photo used for the cover was taken by the author's family. Photo for the back cover taken by the author.

This is a work of fiction. The author's intent is to share stories that have been shared with him by friends and family members. Names will be altered as well as portions of the story lines. However, most of what you are reading will be actual true shared memories.

No part of this publication may be reproduced in any form, or by any means, electronic or mechanical, including photocopying, recording, or any information browsing, storage, or retrieval system, without permission in writing from the publisher.

Published by:

Grape Creek Publishing
P.O. Box 1635
Danville, IL 61834-1635

Table of Contents

Dedication…………………………………………...VI

Forward by the author……………………………VII

Chapter 1 – Memories from "L"…………………..1

Chapter 2 – Memories from "B"…………….…....9

Chapter 3 – Memories from "G"………………...27

Chapter 4 – "R" <u>Encounter with a Doe</u> …………..43

Chapter 5 – "R" <u>Buck in the Garden</u> ……………..51

Chapter 6 – "R" <u>Fishing Stories</u> …………………56

Chapter 7 – "R" <u>Trip Out West</u>……………….…73

Chapter 8 – "R" <u>A Visit with Pop</u> ……………..….78

Chapter 9 – "R" <u>Draw</u> …………………………….85

Chapter 10 – "R" <u>Memories of Canada</u>…………89

Chapter 11 – "R" <u>Ice Sparkles in the Sun</u> ……...96

Chapter 12 – "R" <u>A Shot of Whiskey</u> …………..100

Chapter 13 – "R" <u>Death of a Fawn</u> ……………...103

Chapter 14 – "R" <u>Celebrity Connections</u> ……...106

Chap. 15 – "R" <u>The Mob: It's Who You Know</u>...114

My Reflections - ……………………………….....119

Biography - ………………………………………...122

Dedication Page

I'm dedicating this book:

In Memory of

My dad Donald H. "Bud" Wilson (Pop)

October 18, 1925 to July 6, 2012

To My Father-in-law,

Lowell D. Garner "Garnie"

&

His brother & my uncle by marriage,

Lloyd Eugene Garner "LEG"

"nicknames"

Listening to all three of these men tell their stories, childhood adventures and pranks, hunting and fishing tales, job related moments, and more led me to want to create a compilation of these "Memories"!

Forward

Before I start you on this journey into the past, talking about family memories, childhood episodes, stranger than life events, vacation experiences, and an assortment of other clips into our families I would just like to say that all of this is based on true family experiences. I will classify this book as a fiction writing only because I may not have some of stories 100% accurate in details. The basic stories will be factual but memory – either theirs or mine could have left details out or I may choose to embellish a bit on my own.

My intent here is simply to entertain the reader with stories and events that they themselves may not have had the pleasure to experience. I will say this, the stories referred to as having come from "R" are my shared experiences and are TRUE. Hope you can enjoy the humor in the stories meant to be funny. Open yourselves up to those stories that are unusual and you may find that you also may experience some similar happenings in your own lives.

Chapter 15 I am sharing more as a bit of family history rather than a memory. Because of the historic part this plays on our hometown and also the history of our country I am using the actual names in this account. What I am sharing has already been put into print by a fellow author.

~ Chapter 1 ~

"L"

I guess you find it strange that an old man like me would reflect back on my past like I do but you see it is normal for us to want to remember our roots. It's our roots that make us who we are today. If you have had a bad past then it may be unpleasant to bring these memories up, sometimes even painful. But you see mine are good memories, the kind that can even bring you closer to your family. I am an old man now, soon to be 80 years old. I have had a good, full life and have been fortunate enough to have done a lot of different things through my years.

Now I just like to sit on my porch and drink my cup of coffee and have a puff or two since my wife Betsy doesn't like me smelling up the house with the aroma of burning tobacco. We live in Augusta, Georgia now, bought our house in a subdivision that was built in an old pecan orchard. In the fall, when I am not sitting on my porch relaxing, I walk back and forth through the yard picking up the pecans that drop from our three Pecan trees. You have to be careful though because sometimes they come down with so much force that they can do some damage. We had a neighbor that was killed by one, hit him right on top of his head…who could have guessed a thing like that would happen. Look out, here comes another one!

I've had a number of jobs through my life, liked them all and don't regret a single opportunity I have been given to learn something new. That probably goes back to my childhood helping my Dad with odd jobs to keep our family fed. Like everyone else who lived and grew up through the depression we were poor folks although we didn't know it because we didn't know what it was like to have anything.

I was going to make a career in the military, or so I thought. I joined the Navy when I came of age and was in there for a stay of sixteen years. Then my last four years I was going to put in with the Air Force working with the aircraft but my first wife got sick so I left after just two years. After she passed I went to work for Boeing. There I was caught up in a strange freaky aircraft explosion caused by a grounding error of some kind. It burnt me something terrible, messed up my lungs and stomach…ended up retiring on a Boeing disability. That's water under the bridge now. We can't do anything to change that.

Memories

      We come from Arkansas originally, mainly in the rural parts because Dad always looked for places on the edge of town for us to settle into. That gave us room to put in a vegetable garden and raise some cows and chickens. We always had fresh milk and eggs and occasionally we had fried chicken for supper. As we got older Dad showed me and my brother Dean how to hunt and fish so we would have fresh meat to eat when we got lucky. It took awhile for us boys to get as good at getting the game as our Dad was but the hungrier we got the better shots we got to be with our single shots. The fishing was yet another story, we not only had to learn where the best holes were for catching our fish but also the patience Dad had for sitting on the river bank and waiting for them to bite. Sometimes we lost that battle and went in skinny dipping, it was more fun but then we didn't eat as punishment for not bringing home supper. After a few times of not eating we learned which was more important.

      Times were tough for all back then and jobs were hard to find. Our Dad went around finding odd jobs where ever he could, cutting wood for folks for their cooking stoves and fireplaces if they had one. It really didn't matter what jobs he could find cause he could do just about anything he put his mind to. Folks were more than happy to find things for him to do if they could cause they knew he had seven mouths to feed. We had a fair sized family with Mom, Dad, and the five of us kids. There was me and my younger brother Dean and our three sisters Ellen, Faith and Janet.

There were several times in my growing up when there just was no work to be had and we had to move. Dad said, "We have to go where the work is at and for now that looks like Washington." It was a long trip and we made it three times but there was work to be had. Washington State had a lot of fruit orchards and there was picking to be done. We went from orchard to orchard because harvest time was different depending on what needed to be picked. The work at times was hard but it gave us something to make a living at. Like I said I enjoyed every opportunity to learn something new. It was like an adventure for me, fun and exciting but hard work which left me very exhausted at the end of the day.

Every time we gathered up to move on one of these trips Dad would sell the cows to get money to pay our way and also to pay for a new place once we got there. As I said before, we always looked for a place at the edge of town or even out a ways so we could have ground to put in a garden and raise our livestock. Usually these places were cheaper because nobody in town wanted them knowing they were too far away from all of the places they would want to go. It didn't take long for Dad to come up with new cows and chickens neither.

As I settle back in my porch swing I start to recollect our first trip out west to that far off land they

Memories

called Washington State. I only knew of it from things I had heard people say about it and a few pictures I saw of it. It was strange but also exciting to think we were headed for a new land, hoping to meet up with friendly souls who might become our new friends. We made friends easy no matter where we went cause Mom and Dad made it a rule to do so. They said it was important to have good friends around, helps to keep your spirits up and helped you to grow.

Dad had an old 1929 Model A back then that got us just about anywhere we wanted to go. It was a tight ride though with Dean sitting in the back with our sisters and cousin, I rode in the front with Mom and Dad. Our belongings were tied on as tight as we could get the rope to make sure they survived the trip. We must have looked quite the sight going down the road with all of that heaped onto the old Model A but we were not the only ones on the road with those sorts of circumstances. In amongst our belongings were some crates with our chickens, Dad always figured that Mom could make us something to eat from the eggs and by the time we arrived in the state of Washington we needed to buy new chickens cause we ate ours one by one on the way.

Now growing up Dean and I loved playing little tricks on people, especially Mom. Mom wasn't that much older than us since she was only thirteen when she and Dad got married. Dad was eighteen years old and more than capable of taking care of her. We found out early that Mom only had schooling through the third grade so she didn't know that much as far as reading, writing and arithmetic. She picked up what she could from us as each one of us went to school. Dean and I found out that Mom was a lot of fun to tease, we had to be careful though not to get Dad mad at us or we might end up with a wuppin'.

    Now Mom just loved to do snuff and she had always kept a can with her wherever she was to spit in. On our trips out west she always kept it on the floor board next to her. She would always chew up a big wad of it and her cheeks would be bulging from having a mouth full of that awful juice. Of course then she would reach for her can and spit. It was the worst thing to watch and didn't smell all that great either. On our first trip to Washington I got the idea, a trick we could play on Mom. We stopped at a gas station to get gas and so we could all use their outhouse. Us kids went first and then Mom and Dad used it after Dad got the gas we needed. While Mom was in there I got in the front of the Model A and grabbed the spit can. I hid it carefully so Mom wouldn't notice it when she came back. As soon as we were done we left and got a ways down the road before it happened. Mom had a mouth full of juice she needed to get rid of and started looking for her can. Dad noticed she was looking for something. He then noticed her cheeks bulging and knew exactly what was missing. He looked directly at me and asked, "Where is it?" I told him I took it out at the station so he turned around and headed back. On the way back he found a place to

Memories

pull over so Mom could get out and spit. When he got back to the station we looked and there it was still sitting at the base of the gasoline pump. Dad acted mad about my little joke on Mom but I knew that he thought it was funny also.

We loved playing jokes on Mom because she was nothing more than a big kid herself. We would play one joke after another until she would get mad at us and send us out to get a switch so she could wup us. Dean hated the thought of those switches and he always took off running. She would always send me after him and tell me to be sure and bring a switch back with me. We usually stayed away for hours and by the time we got home she had forgotten what she was going to scolded us for. Mom was unusually ticklish so we together would gang up on her, me on one side and Dean on the other. We could get her laughing so hard that she could not hold it and she would wet on herself. Those were some fun times!

Fun times and yet we had some hard times too. During the time surrounding WWII, there was a munitions factory that went up in our area. One of the many jobs that my Dad did was working in that factory making grenades. He worked in what we thought was a safe environment until the accident happened. The grenades he worked on were made in a huge tank of water so if anything would go wrong then you would be protected from the explosion. Safety was top priority and they had a perfect record until the day of

Dad's accident. It wasn't his fault, not sure it was anyone's fault really…but it happened.

    Dad had his hands inside the work area under the water working on a piece when one slid in underneath his hands and exploded. Never heard for sure what damage anyone else had from it going off, Dad's was bad enough. When you are working on the grenades you really can't wear protective gloves so your hands are going to be exposed to anything that could go wrong. When it exploded, Dad's hands were severely burned. He was rushed to the local hospital where they cleaned up his wounds and then wrapped them up. Both of his hands wrapped past the wrist and were to be that way for over 6 months. Of course Dad couldn't do anything for himself, we had to help him with everything…that's right, everything. We had to follow along with him out to the outhouse and when he was finished we had to take care of him. Well, being the jokers that we were we would play tricks on him like locking him into the outhouse or walking away and leaving him there by himself. He would just sit in there and yell for us. We were off just a laughing until finally we would show up and let him out. He would be mad at us but we knew he couldn't do anything to us…then. Later on when he got better he more than made up for the pranks we played on him. It's a wonder Dean and I ever survived those years, but we did. Good old times they were!

~ Chapter 2 ~

"B"

I grew up in the central part of Illinois and have lived here all of my life. It was Mom and Pop, my older sister Elizabeth, me and my baby sister Jane. I'm an old man now in my eighties and I've had a good life as far as I'm concern. Oh, without doubt there were many who may have been better off than I was but I don't think any of them really had a better life than we did. Growing up Mom and Pop saw to it that we always had food on the table and the essentials for life.

Pop was born and raised around Tuscola, Illinois and came from a family who were all farmers. From the time I was a little squirt, well as far back as I can remember my Pop always had a garden or two which supplied a good portion of our everyday essentials to survive. At one point of my life Pop was gardening three full city lots...I was elected to turn it all over by hand. Every night after school I would be out there turning the dirt over and I was expected to stay with it until it was all done, not in one day of course. But I'm getting ahead of myself, that part of my life came much later.

What I can remember of my younger years, Mom and Pop, my older sister Beth as many of us called her and I all lived in a very small one room garage apartment. It was quite cramped as you can imagine but it got even more so when Mom's brother and some other man I didn't really know at the time came to stay with us. They came and went so that wasn't all of the time but they were family as far as I knew so for me it was fine.

Sometime when I was around four Pop had decided to move us to Indiana. You see there weren't many jobs at that time to be had here at home but there was some big construction going on over in Indiana and it was too far for Pop to travel back and forth. He and Mom decided to just up and move us all over there for as long as Pop had a job. You see Pop was a steam fitter and there was big demand for that on these construction sites. Before our Indiana trip Pop moved us to Kankakee for a short bit. He and a friend got a job putting sewer line across the river there. We lived in tents during the summer but come fall he brought us back home and he along with his friend worked through the winter. They lived in the tents heated by a small wood stove. They worked for a local firm from Urbana who won the bid for that job.

Memories 11

It was the same firm that wanted Pop to go to Indiana on the big construction site there. Yes, Pop was going to be doing the same work there but this time it was not across a river. I will never know how my Pop survived during the winter but he did say they heated bricks and put them in their beds for warmth.

    I don't remember too much of the trip over to this place they were taking us in Indiana but the one thing I never will forget is that time one of our tires passed us on the road. That's right. A trailer tire came loose from the trailer and passed by us. Back then the only road we had to travel on was a rough two lane highway… we didn't have the big super highways that are travelled now. Not far out of town shortly after we left Pop hit a culvert and the jolt popped the tire loose, rim and all. We had too many things to fit in the car with us so Pop got a trailer to haul behind us. The funny part was there was an elderly man going with us, never knew who he was but he had to ride on top of our stuff on the trailer. When the tire came off of the trailer all I can remember in my mind is seeing that tire rolling past us with this man right behind it trying to catch it. We all broke out in laughter at this old man huffing and puffing as he brought back our tire. Of course he didn't see the humor in it.

    We didn't stay over there very long so I don't have a lot of memories of that time. We moved to New Albany, Indiana on September 3, 1929 just before I turned four in October. We came back to

Urbana, Illinois on December 18, 1930 a short time after I turned five. We lived in a small yellow house surrounded by large mounds of dirt. The dirt was from the digging they were doing putting in their sewer pipe. I used to go out with my little lunch box in one hand, shovel in the other and I would dig in the dirt while the men would work. When they stopped for lunch I did too. The one thing I do remember when I got a bit older was during good weather Mom used to fix me lunch in my little lunch box and I would go off to work with Pop. He would sit me up on the hillside above the area where he worked. I was far enough out of the way that I was in no danger but yet I could still see my Pop working. It was just like I was on the job with him and when they would stop for lunch I opened my lunch box and ate along with the guys. Occasionally, when he could Pop would come up on the hill and sit beside me so we could eat lunch together. Once when there were several other workers sitting with us Pop asked me my opinion on how to take care of one particular problem on the site. The men seemed to get a big kick out of my answer. Those were hard times for Mom and Pop, I know that now but I have some really great memories of working with my Pop.

    That yellow house holds one other memory for me. One afternoon while I was playing out front with Beth and a friend of hers a black dog came by. He looked very mean, he had a crazed look in his eyes and we noticed he was foaming around his mouth. I

Memories 13

really didn't understand why but Beth yelled "He's got rabies, run for the house." Now my Mom heard her yell and came running to the front door. When she looked out and saw the dog chasing us she opened the screen door to let us in and stepped between us and the dog. She managed to trap the dog between the screen door and the wall using her broom until we could all safely get into the house. I never knew what happened to the dog, I suppose that after we got in the house it just took off. We never did see it again and I was glad.

Like I said that time didn't last long and once we got back home to Urbana we moved back into our place over by Weber School. I don't really remember anything about where we stayed at that time...I just remember playing on the sidewalk in front of the school. It seems to me that my Mom and Pop found a home for us a short while after that. The man that Pop worked with in Kankakee didn't go with us to Indiana and while we were gone he found out about this place close to another school...Washington. When we got back he told Pop about this house where old man Hatchel lived. Seems that the old man wanted someone to stay with him in the house and take care of him. In exchange, he would leave the house to them when he was gone.

Mom and Pop went to the block where the house sat and looked at it. They both liked the looks of the house and decided to talk with the old man. Now you have to realize that this house was not up for sale, but they wanted it anyway. They went up to the front door and knocked, knocked again and then knocked some more. Finally, this old man came to the door to see what they wanted. They asked him if he would be interested in selling his house to them. He said why don't you young folks come on in and we will talk about it.

He let them in and they sat down with him and discussed why they wanted his house. Well, he didn't want to sell them his house but he made them a very interesting proposition that they both knew ahead of time he would do. He said that he was an old man who lived by himself and if they would move in and take care of his needs such as laundry, cooking, grocery buying, taking him to the doctor when he needed to go, etc. then he would leave them his house. They discussed it over and decided that they would be willing to do that for him so they agreed. Pop took him down to a lawyer who drew up the agreement and they signed it. We all moved in and Mom and Pop took care of him just as they had agreed and he went on to live another five years or so before he passed.

I loved living there in that house, it was so much bigger than we were used to and yet now that I look back at it...it was not really all that big at all. Pop and I at one point dug out underneath the house and put in a basement, as it were. Not a very high ceiling but it added a lot more space. The house was heated by a very small heat stove and it got very cold in the winter time. After we built the basement Pop put in a big boiler which he converted to a coal furnace…we had plenty of heat after that. My Pop could do just about anything he put his mind to. Later, he added a back porch with steps going down to the basement and an indoor bathroom which consisted of basically a closet with a stool and window and that was it. We had a sink beside that little room that we washed up in…but we had it better than many.

We lived just down the street from the school so we had a playground not far from home to play in. My sisters and I used to spend as much time as we could at the school with our friends playing. Oh, I forgot, Mom and Pop gave me another sister a short while after we moved into the house. They named her Jane Marie.

Mom did what she could to help also not only taking care of us kids and doing the housework and cooking for our family but she also took in laundry for others. Sometimes we had to barter different chores for some folks in exchange for doctor bills or buying store goods. I mowed the lawn for the Doc while Pop trimmed his hedge and Mom washed his dirty office laundry. He liked the way she did the wash cause she got everything so white. Doc always brought a basket of freshly picked apples for me to eat and said for me to help myself which I did. They were big and juicy. I have to say that not only did helping my Mom and Pop teach me responsibility but it made me feel very much needed.

Pop continued for quite some time doing odd jobs here and there to keep us going. He did more work for that same firm that he worked for up in Kankakee and over in Indiana. They hired him to help put sewer pipes in underneath the roads both in Urbana and Champaign. As long as they had work for him to do they kept him busy but that too didn't last. Somewhere along the line Pop helped build the Memorial Stadium at the University of Illinois but I don't even know what he did...just know he did it. Eventually he got on at Chanute Air Force Base up at Rantoul using his steam fitter skills. He built, fixed and repaired their heating system up there for years and that was where he was eventually to retire.

As I got older I became good friends with two brothers who lived next door to us. Their dad was a fireman and would leave early each morning to go to the firehouse. After he left their Mom would set them out on the front porch next to the support posts. She tied each of them to a post and told them to stay there and she would untie them when she got back, leaving shortly thereafter. While she was gone they would untie the ropes and go play. They always managed to tie themselves back up before she came back home and she never knew what they had done. I found out later that she was a bit of a rounder and one day their Dad came home early, found out what she was doing and eventually divorced her. When we got older, all three of us were involved with World War II where the

Memories 17

older brother got killed. I was told that he got hit in the head by a sniper, he never knew what hit him.

Later on as I approached my teen years I became very interested in fishing and eventually hunting. My buddies and I would ride our bikes for miles carrying our poles and fishing tackle because there weren't any spots to fish close by. We enjoyed our fishing so much that we didn't mind the ride at all. Mom even helped me make my dough balls and taught me how to make Carp bait with Wheaties. I always wondered how she knew so much about fishing bait but found out when I got a little older that her brothers and the rest of her family all liked to fish also. Maybe that is the reason why I love it so much. While living at home I would sneak off over to the Calvary Grounds which were a part of the local Fair Grounds. It was right beside Crystal Lake Park, our town park and was the best place to shoot squirrels. I would use shorts in my .22 caliber rifle because they were not as loud and nobody would know where I was. My hunting and fishing became a very big part of my life and I was very active with it well into my upper seventies or early eighties. Many times people referred to me as "an old river rat."

Things were so hard while we were growing up that my sisters and I all learned how to do things so we could help around the house. I learned how to do washing and ironing which I benefited from while I was in the Navy. I rarely took any of my shore leave or weekend passes, most of the time I stayed back by myself which I found peaceful. Once the guys found out I was good at washing and ironing they asked me to do theirs for them which I did…for a good price of course. Between the laundry and selling them my extra cigarettes I was able to send home to Mom and Pop a fair amount of my extra money. I didn't have any way of getting an iron so Pop went out, found and bought me one for $5. It was the only one he could find. He mailed it to me and I made good use of it through the rest of my time there in the Navy.

One of my buddies in the Navy worked in the mess hall and sometimes at night while he was cleaning up I would join him. I would sit and drink coffee and talk to him while he was cleaning up and occasionally he would pull something out for us to snack on. I gained over 20 pounds during that time, coming into the Navy I weighed about 113 pounds wet with a 26 inch waistline. I jumped up to a sizable 135 pounds sometimes more. This was not the only time that happened though. While stationed in New York I lived with a Greek family who always ate big meals. The wife would always act offended if you didn't leave the table stuffed so this too became a rough time for me weight wise. I have to say though that she was a really good cook so I sure didn't mind so much stuffing myself. Life in the Navy was different for sure but I had some buddies at that time that became lifelong friends.

One of the most unusual things that happened to me took place at a hunting lodge I went to down in

Memories

Tennessee. The trip consisted of four of us; myself, my wife, a neighbor of ours and his wife. We went to the lodge with the intent of bringing back wild boars. I'm not used to that kind of hunting for sure where the game can actually attack and mame you. In Illinois I'm used to hunting rabbits, pheasants, squirrels, deer and quail. This is a totally different kind of hunting when compared to wild pigs that have tusks that can rip you apart in a heartbeat. Anyway, one night at the lodge I got up early thinking it was time, wrong. Nobody else was up or so I thought. I was sitting in the main sitting room enjoying the fire in the fireplace and admiring the heads hanging on the walls when I was joined by the owner. He was up early to prepare breakfast for the hunters and guides and noticed me sitting in there. He asked me if I would like to join him for some coffee. I of course took him up on his offer because I love my coffee. He talked with me while he prepared the breakfast and I noticed that he kept looking at me. I finally asked him why and he said it was very odd but that I looked just like a fella that he knew years ago. We started asking each other questions until it finally came out that he knew and was good friends with my Uncle Hershel, my mother's youngest brother. He said that I very much resembled him. Looking at pictures of us, both family and friends have said over the years that we could have been twins.

Uncle Hershel, while he was in the service during World War II was stationed at Crossville, TN at a "German Prisoner Camp." He drove an ambulance while stationed there and became good friends with many of the locals around there who invited him to join their Card Club. Hershel was an excellent poker player who did very well at their games. It seems that was where he met this man who was now the owner of the hunting lodge. The owner shared with me that he and my uncle played poker together and he said that my uncle was a natural at it. My uncle actually bought and paid cash for a brand new 1940 Dodge convertible with some of his winnings when he came home from the service. It's funny, the owner said that he was sure that a lot of his losses helped pay for my uncle's car, then he laughed. I was just amazed at meeting him after all of these years, close to fifty years later. Small world!

Memories

~ Most Memorable Navy Experience ~

That would have to be when I was coming back from boot camp and being stationed at a base. I remember passing through Philadelphia at night and thinking those "night lights" were so beautiful. We ended up in Washington D.C. – I can still remember going down Pennsylvania Ave. The one thing that struck me was how pretty and clean it was, the Cherry Blossoms were in bloom and I can truthfully say that I had never seen anything like them before. We found out that the Secretary of the Navy William Franklin Knox had just died (April 28th, 1944)…we all knew him as Frank Knox. He had also been the Republican Vice Presidential Candidate in the 1936 election. We stayed for the funeral and I was given guard duty at the back gate. There was a huge iron fence around the base and at my end is where the ladies barracks stood. It was April and already very hot and I stood at that gate, in full dress blues from 7am until 7pm. With no break or relief I was getting very thirsty. I can remember sometime in the afternoon a couple of the waves were passing by and one of them came over to me and spoke. "It is very hot and you look thirsty, would you like a Coke?" I told her yes and so she went and got me a nice cold Coke which sure hit the spot. To this day I regret not ever getting her name. I sure would like to thank her again for that kindness she showed me all of those years ago. Thank you Ma'am!

~ Most Unusual Thing You've Seen ~

That would have to go back to a time when I was a young adult. In the spring each year we would always prepare for our bank pole fishing for catfish. We usually would seine our minnows in drainage ditches up by Leverett, Illinois…a small railroad stop north of Urbana. Well, being the spring we would have to always deal with the erratic Illinois spring weather which usually means tornados.

This particular year we had already gone through several bouts of rough spring storms with several tornados having passed by locally. I had heard that one did some damage in that area but had not been up there yet to see it firsthand.

There is a nice old farm house on the property where the ditch we go to for our minnows passes through. In the yard, which I would guess to be close to a couple of acres were several very large mature oak trees…one being quite massive. They always kept the yard looking clean, neat and well groomed. Lo and behold, when we got up there and believe me when I tell you we didn't have to be close, it was the most remarkable thing I think I have ever seen. The tornado must have picked up that farm house and sat it down right smack in the top of that huge oak. It was just unbelievable, and of course there were broken branches on the ground but the remainder of that tree was supporting that house. Purely amazing!

~ THE SAILORS LAMENT ~

I am sitting here and thinking of the days I left behind,

And think I'll put on paper what is running through my mind.

People on the outside think a sailor's life is swell,

But I'll let you in on something mate, a sailor's life is hell.

A sailor has one consolation though – gather close and I will tell:

When I die I will go to Heaven because I've done my stretch in Hell.

I've scrubbed a million bulkheads and I've chipped ten miles of paint;

A meaner place this side of Hell I'll swear to you there ain't.

I've stood for endless hours just waiting for my mail,

And I've stood a million watches and been on every special detail.

I've shined a million miles of brass and I've scrubbed my dirty duds;

I've swung a million hammocks and I've peeled a million spuds.

I've cruised a thousand miles and I've made a thousand ports;

I've spent the night in duty jail for trying to be a sport.

But when those final taps are sounded and I lay aside life's cares,

I'll take my final shore leave right up those golden stairs.

"Tis then St. Peter will greet me and loudly he will yell:

"Take your front seat in Heaven, Sailor because you've done your hitch in Hell."

"This poem was a part of my Pop's Navy memorabilia and was printed on a piece of paper with a header which stated: **U. S. NAVAL AIR STATION - PATUXENT RIVER, MARYLAND**

~ "YOU CAN'T WIN" ~

Sailors are what some women marry. They have two feet, two hands, and sometimes two wives; but never more than one dollar, or one idea at a time. Like a Turkish cigarette, all sailors are made of the same material. The only difference is that some of them are a little better disguised than others.

The "Lover" is the one you find surrounded by women. The husband is the one goes ashore in the first boat. The bachelor is the one who has a bank account.

Making a husband out of a sailor is one of the highest plastic arts known to civilization. It requires science, culture, common and uncommon sense, faith, hope, and charity—mostly charity.

If you flatter a sailor you frighten him to death, if you don't you bore him to death. If you permit a sailor to make love to you, he gets tired of you in the end but if you don't he gets tired of you at the start. If you agree with him in everything you soon stop charming him. If you believe all he tells you he thinks you are a dope and if you don't he thinks you are a cynic.

If you wear gay colors, rouge and a charming hat he hesitates to take you out. If you wear a sensible outfit he takes you and stares all evening at the women in gay colors. If you join him at wild parties and smoke with him he swears you are crazy. If you try to reform him he thinks you are treating him as a child.

If you are true to him he doubts you have a brain. If you aren't he longs for a playmate. If you look at other fellows he is jealous. If you don't he hesitates to marry a wall-flower.

If you "high-hat" a sailor he gives you a Bronx cheer and goes right on having a good time. If you treat him civilly and try to cheer him up he gets gloomy and mopes. If you treat him politely he will knock your teeth out and if you are impolite he will call you a heathen. If you take him out to a swell restaurant or some swanky hotel to dine he will drink out of the finger bowl. If you take him to a cheap restaurant he will demand his food served in courses.

<u>"You just can't win"</u>

"This was also among my Pop's Navy memorabilia and I'm not sure where it came from but he told me he had some buddies this sure would have described."

~ Chapter 3 ~

"L"

Well here I am now living alone after losing my lovely wife 10 years ago. We have been happy living some 50 years together and were blessed with three fine kids, two boys and a girl. I spend as much time as I can with my daughter and son-in-law, helping him keep up the mowing on their property in Danville, IL. My boys both live out of the state, the oldest one in Michigan and the youngest in North Dakota. I've had to slow down a bit now that I have past 80 years old and had a few surgeries of my own.

My life started down in Arkansas, my Mom and Dad had five of us kids; two of us boys and three girls. We lived in several different places but most of my earlier life we lived a little ways southeast of Little Rock. Growing up we were always busy doing what we could for our ages. When we got old enough we worked the garden, or chopped wood. We had to cut the wood two different ways. The larger chunks were for the heat stove but we had to cut much smaller pieces for Mom to use in the cook stove. We also helped Mom can a lot of the food we grew in the garden and I always got so tired of this, complaining a lot. My Dad always said, "Yes - but come along next January and February it's going to taste purty good, idn't it?" I had to always agree. We never had any electricity until we moved to Washington State so while we were doing our chores the girls cleaned and filled the kerosene lamps.

We used to find all kinds of mischief to get into as kids. If we could find the right trees to climb, we would climb up the larger trees and then jump over into the top of a smaller tree and ride it down as it bent over from our weight. Always ready to play in the water whether it was a river, pond or whatever…we loved to skinny dip. When we did these sorts of things Dad would always scold us when we got home but rarely did he ever spank us.

I was helping my Mom snap beans getting them ready for canning when I felt a pinch on my back. I figured a fly was biting me and swatted it away. A few minutes later it got me again in a little different spot. I took my flannel shirt off and a Black Widow spider came crawling out. Mom smashed him with a bean to kill him. She sent my brother Larry to go fetch Dad. On the way he met a man on a horse and told him the story. He rode Larry to where my Dad was working and then told Dad to use his horse

Memories

to get back to me. When the doctor got there I was quite sick, he gave me some kind of medication which helped but I guess I was sick for weeks…I really don't remember too much about it.

We used to hang around my uncle's house growing up and there always seemed to be a lot of loose cows, they never bothered us though. Once a bull joined them and he chased us up a tree. We were up there for a couple of hours when we decided to pee on his head which just made him mad. Then we got an idea, pulled out our slingshots and hit that bull right on the testicles. He left us alone after that.

Growing up we had our own bull and when he got big enough we started riding him. We rode him all over the field up until he got to be around 1200 lbs. or so, then Dad decided to sell him. When the man came to buy him, Dad sent us out to go fetch the bull. The man was shocked when we came back riding on him and said if he was that tame with us, he didn't think he'd have any trouble with him. Dad agreed.

When I was around six or seven I was in the kitchen cutting up an apple. Larry kept grabbing for it and I warned him, "You keep it up and I'm going to hack ya." He reached for it again and I got him…laid his thumb wide open. It left a scar that he carries even to this day. Of course I got a wuppin' but not for cutting him, it was for having the knife to begin with. I was told not to mess with the knives.

One day we were playing in a neighbor's barn when I got hurt. I was up in the loft playing in the hay when the others started climbing up after me because I wouldn't come down. I started down the ladder but lost my footing and fell knocking them off on my way down. I hit my head and ended up with a concussion for a few days...don't remember too much from that either.

Before we were to go to town with mom one time we had decided to go over to tease our neighbor, Ben Jay. He was up roofing a shed so we snuck into his Persimmon patch, I called them persimmons but they might have been grapes...I don't remember. Anyway, we started shooting them with our slingshots and hitting him all over. Larry told me to watch him and he took one and knocked Ben Jay's hat off. He hollered, "Alright boys I know who you are and I'll get your Dad after you." We ran home and left for town with Mom. When we got home Ben Jay was there with Dad and looked at us shaking his hand at us. Dad asked us if we had done what he said we did (Dad knew we had because he knew us) but Mom said we couldn't have because we were in town all day with her. There wasn't much Ben Jay and Dad could say to that...whew!

I used to go visit at my Uncle Theodore's place for two or three weeks during the summer time. While he worked, my uncle would always carry a jug around with him and take a swig from time to time. You know I thought that it was water (I was around 8 or 9) and

Memories 31

asked him for a drink, so he handed me the jug. Taking a big slug out of it I nearly lost my breath so I asked him what it was. He said, "White lightning, boy." He laughed. I wanted no more of that stuff. On that same visit I saw him smoking, he rolled his own (Bull Durham I think) so I asked him what that tasted like. He handed me one and I took a big puff and again it took my breath away. I wanted no more of that either.

Another time at Uncle Theodore's a few years later he went a hogging after wild hogs, in the fall I believe. He looked at me and said, "Now boy don't you be gettin' off this wagon you hear me?" "I won't!" I didn't neither cause them hogs got mean. They used to make sausage and can it. Then they would smoke the hams and the rest of the meat. In later years he told a story where they had gone out hunting rabbits. At this particular time they had some hogs of their own in a fenced in area. One of the guys was tired so he stopped awhile to rest while the rest went on. He must have climbed up on the hog fence to rest, fell in and hit his head knocking him out cold. When the others came back they found him in the hog lot with the hogs eating on him. His face was mostly gone. I wouldn't even get around them hogs after that.

Now we had an Aunt Belle who was a large woman, over 200 lbs. She was also a very big busted woman…she loved to hug kids. Well sir, whenever she was around we would shove each other to see who she was going to hug first. She would grab one of us and wrap her arms around ya and squeeze, your face buried between them two big boobs. I'd yell at her, "Aunt Belle…I can't breathe, you're smothering me." She would finally let you go but she always did that.

I remember growing up that whenever we would get a big cut on feet or really most anywhere, when she could mom would have us get cow urine to put on it. I don't know for sure, I guess it was the ammonia in it that healed your cut…sure worked. Mothers who were nursing often would squirt some of their milk into the baby's ear if it had an ear ache, which also seemed to work. If we happened to be in the kitchen with a bad cut mom would often reach into the cook stove and grab some smut (soot), mix it with whatever grease she happened to have there, that always stopped the bleeding as well.

I just remembered that one time while we were doing some canning we used the water hose and forgot to put it back up. Mom went out after dark to do something and stepped right on that hose. She yelled, grabbed her broom and started beating it. Dad came out and asked what she was doing. "I'm a beatin' this shere snake!" she said. Dad replied to her, "Woman, that's a water hose." She stopped swinging her broom plum tuckered out. Mom was only fourteen when they got married and never had much schooling growing up. She learned most of what she knew from us going to school.

Memories

Out on what they used to call the farm Mom and Dad raised chickens and they had this one old banty rooster that used to attack or harass Dad in some way. Just before they were getting ready for a move Dad decided to get rid of some of the chickens. He also decided to get rid of that rooster and have him for supper. Grabbing the rooster with both hands he started ringing its neck which caused the rooster to crap all over Dad's face. Mom laughed and said, "He got even with you even to death!" At that same farm they had a Shetland pony that had been a stud but they had him fixed. After he got fixed he became a bit ornery biting and pinching Dad. Dad was out working on some irrigation pipes one afternoon when that pony came up and bit him on his backside, Dad turned around and hit him right across the nose. He settled down after that.

My older sister was dating, she and her boyfriend came in kinda late one night and Mom said, "It's late and there's no light out there, why don't you just spend the night…you can sleep with the boys." He said okay and spent the night. Now growing up I was a bed wetter, sometime through the night I wet the bed and somehow it got on him. He woke up all excited yelling, "Hey, Hey…what's a going on here?" When he found out what had happened he settled down but we always joked about it later.

My Dad was a railroader by trade but around World War II he worked in a hand grenade factory. He actually made the grenades. They did the work with the grenades under water because of the liquid that is in the grenades. Somehow, one of them moved in and got underneath the one Dad was working on. It triggered and blew hitting Dad's hands, face and some on his chest. Others were injured also but not like dad. When my mother heard the sirens go off she stopped everything she was doing and listened. She said, "Something is wrong, I can feel it." Within a short time someone came to our door and told her Dad had been seriously hurt. They doctored him for quite some time…his hands were like raw meat to start out with. They had this salve that they put on them 6 to 8 times over the months until finally they told him they were going to leave them open, without bandages. He was not to use them for a week but after that he could start slowly to use them again. He could not grip very well for a long time but that slowly came back also. We had to do everything for him and when he would pee sometimes I would shake it to many times and he'd say, "Alright, now put that thing back in my pants quit horsing around." We loved teasing during that time because he couldn't do a thing about it, he made up for it later though. His healing process took over a year.

When Dad got back to working I remember him telling Mom one day, "We are going to have to go where the work is. I am going to move us out to Washington State cause' I can always get a seasonal job there to get started." This was back just coming out of the depression, World War II had created some

Memories

jobs but most areas were still pretty poverty stricken. Dad went down where you get the rationing stamps and talked to them. He explained to them, told them we were moving to Washington and talked them into giving us enough stamps to do so. At that time there were stamps for gas depending on your need, sugar, meat, flour, etc. When we actually got to Washington Dad said he only had enough stamps left for 5 or 6 gallons of gas. I have always wondered even to this day how we ever made it…we did though.

Getting ready for our move was an adventure in itself. Do you remember or have you seen **"Grapes of Wrath"** about them all moving out west. That was pretty much us. My Dad took a long board and fastened it across the two fenders on the driver's side of his 1929 Model A so he could have a place to stack all of our belongings. When we got ready, all eight of us climbed in by the passenger side of the car. Dad, Mom and my brother Larry sat up front. In the back was my three sisters Ellen, Faith, Janet, our 17 yr. old cousin David and myself.

The first night of travel found us camped in a roadside park somewhere in Texas. Later in the afternoon on the second day we ran into a very large thunder storm with lots of lightning so Dad parked us under a bridge. After the storm, water was running off the bridge making quite a racket. David had fallen asleep, woke up to the running water and asked mom, "Aunt Pearl, are you frying taters?" I guess that he wasn't awake yet.

The next day Dad had heard something that didn't sound right with the engine so he stopped to fix it. Us two boys along with our cousin decided to climb this long hill beside the road so we could go to the bathroom. We found a sign lying on the ground at the top of the hill and our cousin said that he would hold it for us and then we could hold it for him. We agreed, and did our thing first. When it was his turn we grabbed the sign and he got himself ready. At just the right time Larry looked over at me, smiled and winked, together we dropped the sign and ran. David came down the hill mad and went to Dad. "Uncle, did you see what your boys did to me. He then proceeded to tell Dad about the incident…to which Dad said he'd take care of it. Later Dad told us, "Now you boys know that wasn't the right thing to do…but I think that was funny."

Somewhere along the trip we had stopped at a gas station to get gas and go to the bathroom. While we were there my brother hid my Mom's spit can at the station and later when she needed it she didn't have. It got pretty funny watching her go a looking for that can…the expression on her face with a mouth full to spit. Later he played another one on her during a rain storm. Larry had seen a flash of lightning and knew in a second or two it would thunder. Just before it did he turned to Mom and went "BANG"…scared Mom so bad she wet her pants.

When we finally got out to Washington state, found a place to live, Dad went and found work with

Memories   37

the fruit harvest. We picked everything from cherries, apples, pears, you name it…they grew it and we picked it. After we were there awhile we learned how to work the Hoppes fields. The spring was spent preparing the fields with wires and strings, when they were ready we started training the plants. Training was simply working them up the strings when they got big enough to do so. At the end of the season we all had our own jobs to do which consisted of cutting the strings in order to be able to harvest the hoppes. From there they went in to be spread out and dried and then bagged to go to the buyers.

      After a couple of years doing this I remember my Dad telling Mom, "This ain't no life for us. I need to do something else – I'm a railroad man." You see my Dad has always considered himself a railroader even though he's had many other jobs. In Arkansas he was working as part of a section gang making repairs. Then before we left to go out west he moved us to Pine Bluff where he did brakeman work. I always thank my Dad for moving us way back then from Arkansas to Washington, he got us away from the poverty we lived in down there. Getting back to the story, Dad had heard that they were hiring brakemen in Walla Walla so he told Mom, "I'm going to talk with them and when I come back I will have a job." Dad left and was gone for ten days. They hired him right on the spot and put him right to work. While he was there he found us a house to rent. He worked ten days straight and then had a couple of days off so he came and got us. We spent those couple of days moving to our new place in Walla Walla. Things sure seem to get better after that. This was the first time I can remember us ever having electricity.

When I got old enough I joined the Air Force. I had several jobs being that I was in for twenty years but I finally made it to the flight lines, worked a lot on the planes and dealt with the fuels. At one point I found myself stationed at Chanute Air Force Base in Rantoul, IL. It was while I was here that I met the love of my life who later became my wife, Jan. My buddy at the base asked me if I wanted to go into the big city meaning Champaign and I said okay I'd go with him. Well there he drove to a place down town known as Grants which was a good size department store. In the store they had a nice large soda fountain and there just happened to be two girls behind it. We started talking to this one and then all of a sudden he went down and started talking with the other one, Jan. We asked if they wanted to go for some hamburgers and cokes at The Pines on south Neil St. We ended up taking them at least four or five times over the next two weeks. I had been given my new orders and was getting ready to leave to my base and told them that. Jan took me over to the side and whispered in my ear, "Why don't you come in tomorrow and we can spend some time together before you go." I said, "All right, I can do that." The next day we spent together talking, getting to know each other & then I took her out for supper. We ended up in Crystal Lake Park,

Memories

parked and did some more talking. It was July but for some reason it was a bit cool so we had the windows most of the way up. We were deep into our discussion when we heard a tap on the window. I rolled it down to see what was up and there was a cop standing there. He asked, "What are you two doing?" I said, "Just sitting here talking officer, why?" "Are you aware that the park is closed at 11:30?" "No sir, what time is it now?" "Midnight." "Oh we're sorry officer." "There is no problem, just find somewhere else to talk that's not in the park." He left and so did we. Before I took her back home I asked her if she wanted to come to the new base with me. She asked, "What do you mean?" "As my wife, I guess I'm proposing to you…do you want to marry me?" She accepted.

The following two days were filled with making preparations for our wedding on Friday afternoon. I already left the base knowing I was transferring to the new base so I got myself a motel room for the next couple of days. After our wedding they gave us a party at her parents' house which was on the east side of Urbana. Now her old man and brothers love to turtle hunt and they had several in this concrete pool in the backyard. Prior to our wedding they had gotten a hold of a big one…I'd say that he wouldn't fit into a #2 washtub. They had to put a sheet of plywood over the pool with concrete blocks on top because he kept crawling out. They fixed him for our wedding dinner with all sorts of goodies to go with him. I figure that he fed 30 to 35 people with leftovers that were eaten the following week…now that's one big turtle. After the party Jan and I spent Friday night at the motel. On Saturday we went back to her parents' house to pack up all of her belongings and then Sunday we left for my new base at Moses Lake. Jan had a boy named Mickey who was a year and a half old. Took him a little while to get used to me but once he did he was just like my own boy.

We were at Moses Lake a short while when I realized that Mickey's tricycle had a squeak. I was getting ready to fix it when Jan stopped me, said that the noise helped her know where he was and when he took off. Mickey took to liking this older couple down the street from us and every morning he would ride his tricycle down to their house. The old man would split a banana for breakfast with him. There was another older woman he found that liked to give him homemade cookies, she spoiled him…but he was still a good kid.

While we lived there in Moses Lake we got a call from my brother Larry. He wanted us to meet him at Union Gap, from there we drove to where our Mom and Dad were…they had a serious accident. Larry and I switched off driving but Jan wasn't comfortable with his driving our car through the mountains so I did most of it. We found out a bus had hit them from the back hurting Dad's neck. Mom was okay even though she had been thrown up into the dashboard next to the windshield. Their car was still drivable so when they were ready to go home Larry drove their car and

Memories

we were in ours. Mom and Dad rode home on an airplane which Mom wasn't used to. She got scared on the plane whenever it would get bumpy and ended up peeing on herself three times, poor Mom had a rough time of it. Dad wore that neck brace for about a year but ended up being okay.

At Moses Lake we used to go to a nearby park with our neighbors at the end of each month. We all pulled together what leftovers we had and had one big picnic. The lake was good for swimming and I decided it was time to teach Mickey how to swim. Jan was not crazy about the idea because she had a fear of the water herself and was afraid he would drown. I got him to try it and after a while he was doing just fine, I could never get her to go any farther than waist deep and that was it. Every once in a while we would drive to Union Gap so I could help during Dad's healing process from the neck injury. That lasted most of that year he wore it.

I got orders to go to Japan and was there for twenty two months during which time my little girl was born. A Western Union telegram came which read, "Baby girl - both doing fine." I took the note to my supervisor and said, "What do you think of that?" He replied, "I think we ought to celebrate." And celebrate we did…two days of it. I didn't know or remember a thing about those two days either. It wasn't until she was thirteen months old before I got back home to see her.

After I retired from the military we came back here to Champaign/Urbana so we could help take care of Jan's Mom. She lost her Dad during my time in the military which was hard on her being away from her Mom when she was needed most. I got a job at the apartments where we lived as a maintenance man for about a year and a half. Then I acquired a job working for an alarm company where I stayed until I retired twenty five years later. When the owner first tested me for the job he was surprised at what all I actually knew about the job. He said, "You're pretty smart aren't ya." To that I replied, "My Dad told me growing up to do a lot of listening, don't talk too much and you will learn more. That's what I did." I enjoyed working for him, he was a good boss and we got along well together.

Well that is about it for me. If someone was to ask me about my life I guess what I would say is this, "I've had an enjoyable life and a lot of bumps, bruises, and hard times…most of it's been good. I'm not really complaining, I don't think I would change a thing if I had to live my life over. Well, yes I would to. I would have paid more attention in school!"

~ Chapter 4 ~

"R"

Encounter with a Doe

There have been several times that I have been asked *"What is your happiest or most rewarding experience in the woods?"* You see I am a hunter, grew up a hunter and have enjoyed it all of my life. It has been very fulfilling for me on so many levels. The actual taking of the game I was after was merely an added plus. While I was growing up the wild game was a large portion of our staples. I am thankful to my father for bringing me up in this environment because it allowed me time to get to be out in nature, to enjoy the beauty that surrounds us. It wasn't till later that I came to realize where this beauty of nature actually came from…God!

After our marriage, my wife and I joined our church Sunday School class every spring on camping trips down to southern Illinois. It was our age group at that time of young adults and we all enjoyed spending time in nature. I think it was the combination of my hunting trips and these camping trips that we actually took down to the same area I hunted, that taught me the peace I feel now while being out "in the woods." Never really thought about it much when I was younger but drawing closer to God as I got older I believe helped me to appreciate what he has provided for us.

It wasn't until 1989 when we bought our property that I really was given the thrills that I try to share with my friends as much as I can now. Our land consisted back then of 23 acres; half farm ground and half woodlands. We had a farmer who took care of the farm ground rotating crops of corn and soybeans year after year. I slowly over a period of time took bits of the land away from him and changed it by planting more trees. At the time of this story though, it would have been early in the 1990's and he was still planting all of the farm ground at that point.

We had a neighbor who actually lived at the very end of our shared private drive. My wife and I first met him when we were looking to buy the property. He allowed us to enter the woods through his place. It was a blessing for us, we couldn't go through the field because at that time it was late summer and the field was a tall stand of corn. Our neighbor lived in a log cabin, a rustic two room old log cabin. He told me later that when he first found the cabin it was a barn with cows in it. He kicked the cows

Memories 45

out and converted the barn into the two room cabin which he then took over. I went into it once and saw that he had a kitchen and a living room.

 A year or two later, in the spring I saw our neighbor out in his field so I went over to talk to him. While we were there talking a little fawn walked up to him. I thought it strange, very strange because that is just not something that happens all of the time. A wild animal usually doesn't walk right up to a person, just where was its mother? Then my neighbor explained to me that the fawn had been orphaned at birth so he took it in and took care of it so of course it looked at him as its mother. I was not only amazed and truly shocked, you might say I was also very envious of his relationship with this little wild creature. He had me hold my hand out and the fawn brushed her nose against my hand and then licked it. He told me as long as he was there she would let strangers touch her, but only when he was around.

 It happened to me late that fall just before deer hunting season. My farmer had already gotten the corn out so the only thing in the field was the corn stubble. I was out in woods looking for deer signs, doing some of my pre-hunt scouting. I just came out of the woods when I saw it. The deer looked to be a doe standing over not far from where I parked my truck…clear across the field. I really couldn't believe that it didn't run when it saw me. The doe stood there just looking at me so I began talking to it, calling to it, trying to entice it to come to me. Right, like this wild doe is going to come right over to me, but she did. Wow! I couldn't believe it.

I know I had to have a look of bewilderment on my face because I went into shock. Here I was calling to this young doe and she slowly made her way straight to me. Now she took her time and walked slow, very slow with her nose in the air and her ears twitching back and forth. Her tail, a big white flag as it were, was waving side by side but it never went up in alert mode which means she was being cautious but never really scared of me. I kept calling and motioning my hand for her to come and she never turned or got side tracked, she made a beeline straight at me. Closer and closer she came and I kept thinking at any minute now she is going to come to her senses and take off running. I didn't time it but I'll bet it took her ten to fifteen minutes to cross that field, for me it seemed a lifetime. My heart was pounding from the excitement. I thought it would explode the closer she got. She was about five feet away when she stopped.

I looked into her eyes and she returned the look, blinking her eyes as she stared. Very slowly I held out my hand and then called to her, "It's okay. Come on girl." She looked at me and then inched closer and closer to me until her nose brushed my hand. I tried to touch her and she pulled back. It wasn't until that very moment that I realized, realized for the first time that this was my neighbor's doe. That was why she came to me, she knew who I was from before when she saw me with him. I remembered

Memories

what he said about the fact that she would only allow someone to touch her if he was around.

There have been those through the years that have asked me, "How can you shoot those pretty deer with those big brown eyes?" You know I have never been close enough to a deer to see into their eyes, at least not until now. And no, if you really want to know the truth I could not have shot her after having looked into her eyes. She spoke to me with her eyes, so gentle and unknowing like she didn't have a care in the world. If I blinked she seemed to blink.

We had this interaction between us for five or ten minutes and I enjoyed every minute of it. Then all at once, she turned and started walking away. No warning and she didn't seem alerted to anything, I think she was just done. Maybe she just wanted to come over and say hi friend. Just like she came, she left walking back across the field. When she reached the far end of the field she stopped and turned back to look at me. It was as if she was saying good-bye to me so I raised my hand to her and said, "Good-bye girl." She turned and with the flip of her tail went through the opening and suddenly she disappeared. What a moment that I will never forget for the rest of my life. Unfortunately, there is one of those – "the rest of the story" endings.

For the next couple of years my neighbor realized that come every fall deer hunting season his doe was going to be a target for all of the hunters in the woods...he hunted also. Determined to do what he could to protect her, one year he tried to spray her hide with bright orange glow paint but that didn't work, the paint rubbed off as she went through the woods. The next year he designed a wreath that he hung around her neck. I guess he figured that anyone who saw her with that wreath around her neck would not shoot her. So far through the bow hunting season it seemed to be working because she was still around. Then a big buck came into the area and she started hanging around with him. All of a sudden she wasn't showing up, we were not sure if she had gotten killed or if she just ran off with him into another area. My neighbor was a bit worried I could tell, to tell you the truth I was also.

Well it finally came, the first season for shotgun hunting. Our deer hunting with firearms in Illinois is split into two three-day seasons, the first one being at the end of November and the second one at the beginning of December. I was hunting by myself that year because the rest of my family was still hunting

Memories

down in southern Illinois. I choose a spot I was going to hunt and was there just before daylight that first morning. About an hour after sun-up I heard a noise on the ridge up the hill from me. I looked and saw the silhouettes of three deer on the top of the ridge that appeared to be feeding. Whitetails just love to eat the acorns, one of their main food staples. The front one appeared to be a buck with a nice rack. I waited for my opportunity and when he was in the opening, I took my shot. A very long shot at that, but I knew I hit my mark…unfortunately.

The other two deer ran out of the woods but the one I shot ran down into the ravine beside me and came my way. As it came by running I took another shot but missed. I saw the wound on the deer as it passed by and knew I made what would be a fatal shot. Then I saw it, the wreath my neighbor placed on his doe was on my deer. Yes that's right, I shot her by mistake…but how? The wreath he put on her at the angle of my shot had parts sticking out that made it look like she had antlers, who would ever have guessed that could happen. I followed her to where she crossed the creek and fell on the other side. She died in sight of my neighbor's cabin.

I didn't have the heart to tell him what happened, and never did. I stood over her and tears came from my eyes…my heart was broken. I should have buried her right there but I was taught at a very early age not to waste what I shoot. But I couldn't take her home with me because I knew I would never be able to eat her. So I got her out of the woods and into my truck without anyone seeing me. I took her home and got in touch with my father-in-law who came over to our house. Together we took her over to my wife's cousin who said he would take her. That had to be the worst day of my life and even to this day I feel my heart breaking when I think of my encounter with the young doe!

~ Chapter 5 ~

"R"

Buck in the Garden

      I grew up in a family of gardeners, as I'm sure many have done. My grandpa on my father's side of the family came from farmers down around Tuscola, IL way. Grandpa I'm sure had his hands into the soil at a very early age. When my Pop was growing up as a young teenager on up, he spent his days after school turning over the ground in grandpa's garden which took quite a while because at one time grandpa had three city lots in garden. Pop got very good at using his pitchfork breaking up that ground, even into his later years. When my mother wanted her garden turned over each spring Pop would breakout his pitchfork even though he had access to a tiller.

      My grandmother on my mom's side of the family also put up a sizable garden. I remember growing up and going over to her house to mow the grass, seeing grandma out in the garden more than once killing the snakes. That freaked me out back then because we never really saw many snakes where we lived in Champaign, IL. Both of my grandparents lived in Urbana not far from the Carle Hospital and Clinic.

  Growing up as a boy in Champaign in a family of seven, my Mom kept up with the tradition she knew as a child. She also put out a garden but it was on a smaller scale than either one of my grandparents' gardens. I was thankful for that because I was the one that had to turn it over with what else, Pop's pitch fork or spading fork. I didn't hate many things but I hated that job. Pop went in halves with my Grandpa on the cost of a tiller but it was at grandpa's house and Pop would never go over to get it for me to use. No, I could do it by hand.

  Once I got married and got my own house, my wife and I put in our own garden. Well I didn't have the extra funds to purchase a tiller so once again it was to be done by hand but I managed to survive it though. We had a garden for many years and I always turned it over by hand but when we moved to our property out in the country things changed. My mother-in-law passed a few years ago and my father-in-law has been very gracious about helping us with the purchase of things he knew would help me with my "chores" as I call them. He went halves with me on a tiller and it was one of the best purchases I have ever made, I just love it.

Memories

Our garden on our new place that we have dubbed "Grape Creek Acres" is much bigger. One, we have the space to put in any size I want to…I'll be honest and say the largest size I feel like managing. Two, I have a tiller and turn it over and over to get it good and broken up, it's great. I try to work it as diligently as I can but sometimes too much rain can prevent me from weeding and it has gotten away from me a couple of times.

However, on this year we had a beautiful garden and everything was growing abundantly. We put in four different varieties of tomatoes all doing great, taters, watermelons, cantaloupe, green beans, cucumbers and of course sweet corn. I had three rows of sweet corn with stalks just bursting with luscious large ears coming very close to time to be picked. Being out in the country we have had to put a fence around the garden to keep the critters out. The deer have learned that they could reach over the fence and get ahold of the outermost ears of corn much to my…well let's just say I didn't like that they figured that out. I tried to put things around the garden to scare them off, all of which failed.

One morning after my wife went to work I went out to check the garden as I usually did on my days off. As usual our tomatoes were growing like wildfire and there were many ready to be picked. The tomato plants were just inside my little door I had rigged to get into the garden and at the far end of the garden was the corn which was standing well over six foot,

I'm five foot five. The early morning breeze was causing the long dry leaves on the corn stalks to pop and crack as they waved across each other. The birds had brought new life to the morning with their lovely chirping, whistling and an occasional screech from the buzzards flying over checking the ground for their next meal. I walked over, entered the garden and checked the plants out. After checking out all of the overwhelmingly full tomato plants I decided to go back into the garage to get a bucket to put those juicy red buggers in and then came back out to the plants to start picking. I heard the hypnotic tones of a flock of local geese as they passed overhead, much like they do every morning. When I bent over to grab some of the lower ones I passed gas. Now this was not silent by any means but a "loud explosion" which must have woke the neighborhood.

 All of a sudden there was all kinds of disturbed commotion behind me in the corn. I turned around just in time to see the large massive form of a ten point buck leaping over my red fence and bound across our back yard slipping into the timber. I would have liked to have seen the look on my face but better still I would have loved to have seen the startled buck's first reaction to my "explosion". He must have been there standing quietly in the corn the whole time I was walking around, going back and forth between the garden and the garage. He had to be watching me and wondering when to make his move. I believe that I decided that for him.

Memories

    I still to this day can see that image of the big buck leaping out of our corn and over the fence in one flawless bound. His dart across the backyard played in slow motion within my head because I was glued to his large rack, mesmerized. What a beauty! Again, that is just one of the joys we have experienced living in the country.

~ Chapter 6 ~

"R"

Fishing Stories

    My Pop really loved his fishing and did so at a very early age. As a teenager he and his buddies would grab their fishing gear, jump on their bikes and ride for miles to fish. As he grew older his desire to fish grew also. You might go so far as to say that when they coined the phrase "old river rat" they were looking at him. When each of us boys came along we naturally were blessed with that same love.

    As Pop matured his desire to catch fish grew. With a family of seven mouths to feed you might say it became a matter of survival. Pop turned to a style of fishing known as "bank poling" which can vary with each fisherman. He purchased a form of bamboo poles that were somewhat similar to cane poles. He and my uncles would rig the poles in a special way that worked best for the way we like to fish.

Memories

It became a weekend ritual every weekend from spring clear up into late fall to head down to the river to bank pole. We ended up having about five spots along the river we liked to fish. Pop learned over the years which spots produced the best results at certain times of the year. We are primarily fishing for catfish although we caught a lot of crappie, perch, and bass. When he first started fishing this way it was just Pop and some of my uncles or even some of his friends or neighbors. When us boys came along it dwindled down to Pop, an uncle, my older brother and occasionally my cousins. When I got old enough I was added to the mix.

On the weekend this story takes place it was my Pop, my uncle and his two sons (my cousins), my older brother and I. Early afternoon we went up to a drainage ditch north of town and seined for minnows, our preferred bait. Once we got to the river my Pop and uncle grabbed their bank poles and each headed his own way, my uncle going up river and my Pop going down river. The rest of us stayed back at camp.

My brother and one of my cousins were playing cards in the front seat of Pop's Ford Country Squire Station wagon. My other cousin was sitting in the back seat watching. For me, it was my assigned task of gathering wood for the campfire. I was really good at gathering wood but had never been taught how to light a fire. Ought to be simple right…wrong. I was soon to learn a very valuable lesson. I was around ten years old when I started fishing and one of my chores at home was burning garbage in our burn barrel. You would have thought I could handle a campfire.

After gathering a really substantial amount of limbs and twigs, and some larger pieces of tree debris, I decided I would try to lay a fire. I put down several sizable pieces of wood thinking it would give me a good start for my fire. I got hold of several scrapes of paper having seen others start fires this way. I lit the paper and watched it burn and it started one of my chunks of wood but the wood didn't keep burning. It just smoldered and smoked which only frustrated me. I looked around and saw a can of gas used for Coleman lanterns. I grabbed the can and undid the cap on the top. Holding it over my wood I started to pour it on the smoking wood. What I was unaware of was some of the wood had some live embers and you guessed it, the whole works went up into flames. I am still holding the gas can which is now on fire also so it was burning my hand. I got scared and toss it.

You don't want to forget the fact that while I am doing all of this my brother and cousins are sitting in the car playing cards. When I threw the can I wasn't aiming for anywhere in particular, I was just scared and wanting to get rid of it. As luck would have it, it landed under the backend of my Dad's car. I yelled which caused the three inside to look my direction. My brother said as they looked out the back of the wagon that all they could see were flames…he thought the car was on fire. They got out of the car and my brother managed to get the can out from underneath the car and he tossed it away from the car.

Lucky for me the car was unharmed but my hand was burned. We all knew I was going to be in big trouble when Pop got back. It wasn't long before he and my uncle were coming back to camp on the trail that led from the river. My brother made me tell Pop my whole story knowing how difficult that in itself would be. Once he checked the car out and was satisfied that it was going to be okay, Pop came back over to me. I could tell that my uncle and all three of the others were waiting for him to lay into me knowing I deserved it. Pop surprised me that day by saying no he wasn't going to spank me. He felt that my burnt hand, the scare I got and the lesson I learned that day was punishment enough. He was right about that but I still appreciate to this day the fact that my Pop had an understanding and loving heart. At a later date he taught me the proper way to lite that campfire.

On an earlier fishing trip before I started going with them, Pop was on a weekend trip with my Uncle Mack, his oldest son and my older brother Lee who was around twelve at the time. At this particular spot there was an old iron bridge right by camp were the road crossed the river, it wasn't one of our more private spots. The river was quite deep right here so we used the bridge to cross over to the other side. As always, my uncle seemed to like going up river so Pop went down the river. Like every other trip the majority of the fish caught was done so by my Pop. My uncle worked very hard at his fishing but just didn't seem to be very lucky at it. This night was a rough night of fishing though because it rained which made the river bank very slippery.

    I am not aware of much of the story as far as to how the night went but as most rainy fishing trips go it probably wasn't all that enjoyable. We usually spent most of the time around the campfire telling stories, reliving past fishing trips or even some old hunting trips. When it rains however, we spent time back at camp inside our cars. It just really isn't near as much fun as being around that fire. They still managed to have a successful night of fishing because come morning they had two stringers full of fish. The stringer in the water had eleven on it which is what they caught through the night. The stringer from their daylight run had five on it and Pop set them in a bucket of water instead of in the river. Now Pop got in the habit of keeping the larger fish separate from the smaller ones because he found that while they were in the water the larger fish moved around a lot and sometimes would break the smaller ones free from their latch. This was not the case here though. It

Memories

seems that they had all of the ones caught through the night on that one stringer.

As the story goes, or at least the way I can remember it being told while they were breaking camp getting ready to head home my brother decided he would help Pop by getting the fish out of the water. I can imaging much like myself Lee probably wore a pair of tennis shoes which would have made it that much more difficult getting up and down that river bank. As he reached down and grabbed hold of the stringer with the larger number of fish Lee slipped and fell, dropping the stringer back into the water. He sat there for a moment shaken from the fall and then it came to him that the fish were now loose in the river, still on the stringer but not attached to anything on the bank now. He blurted out "Ah SHIT" to which my Pop responded with "What's wrong kiddo?"

Pop came over closer to my brother to make sure he was okay when Lee explained to him that he dropped the fish into the river. Lee was lucky because our father's attention was pulled away from him to the fish that were somewhere floating in the river. They got poles and worked them around in the river hoping to snag the stringer. Finally, Pop jumped into the river and felt around but the river was both too deep and the current was swift enough that they had probably been pulled a ways down river by this time. Their attempts to recover that stringer were unsuccessful.

Our uncle became furious at my brother for his unsuccessful retrieval of the stringer, mad at the fact that the night's catch was lost. Pop, though was a little more even tempered about it. Even though he was mad about the loss of most of the fish, he did point out that they still had the other stringer with five nice cats on it in the bucket. He also pointed out the fact that he was the one who caught most of the fish anyway (in a recent memory of that story he said he caught all of them) so if anyone should be angry it should be him. My uncle calmed down and let it be. The only thing Pop said to my brother was that he wished he had spoken up sooner about losing the string because it would have given them more of a chance to get them back. All I can say is that I'm sure glad it wasn't me…this time.

One of our favorite spots to fish actually is off of Route 10, a two lane highway. There is an old metal bridge that went over the river and we usually made our camp under the bridge right next to the huge concrete support for the bridge. I loved this spot because just a short ways from where we camped was a turkey farm and you could hear them on occasion up in the barn gobbling. If it would blow up a

Memories 63

storm while we were here the turkeys would go absolutely crazy. I heard that storms scared them so much that they would jump into a pile, one on top of another and just keep it up smothering all of the turkeys trapped on the bottom of the pile.

On this particular night we started out camping under the bridge but after Pop set out his "bankpoles" and got back to us it blew up a huge storm from the west. We could hear it thundering, first in the distance but it didn't take long for it to work our direction. The wind picked up, trees were swaying back and forth and dust was blowing from out of the fields. Pop knew what was coming so he yelled to us boys to gather our stuff and head for our station wagon. The wind was blowing so hard it was all we could do to get to the car without being carried away.

We just made it into our car parked on the shoulder of the two lane. Wave after wave of the drenching rain battered the windows so hard it sounded as though they would break. It was loud on the inside from the pounding the roof was getting. Pop talked to us boys to get our minds off of the storm but he knew it was a bad one. It worked for a while, every time the lightning struck though it would grab our attention.

My younger brother had fallen asleep before the storm settled down enough for Pop to venture out. It was just before midnight when he decided that he should go check on the poles. He told me to lock the doors while he was gone mainly because where we had to park was on the narrow shoulder of this two lane highway. He made his way down to the river and managed to check most of the poles on our side of the river before crossing over to the other side. He could already tell that the river was rising from all of the rain that had come down.

After he checked what he could on the other side he was heading out of the timber and into a large band of horseweeds that covered an area probably half a block long. These horseweeds are well over our heads but are normally not a problem because we had broken a trail through them. The rain and gusting wind however hid the trail and in a short distance Pop had gotten turned around. The lights we use are old Carbide lights that have a lit flame providing our light, normally working great. Unfortunately one of the wet weeds put out Pop's light and he couldn't get it going again.

Without light he was lost in the horseweeds, aimlessly wondering in the dark. Then he got the bright idea just to listen to the traffic on the highway to help him get his bearings. Problem was that this was the middle of the night and there was no traffic on the highway, none at all. So, all he could do was just stay put and wait the storm out until daylight. Just before daylight, while Pop was still in the weeds lost a State Policeman stopped by to check and see why our car was sitting on the shoulder, apparently stranded. He checked the car out and noticed my brother and me in the car asleep. He tried to open the doors but of course we had the doors all locked.

He hung around until daylight when he evidently saw Pop walking at the far end of the bridge. He met him at the halfway mark and asked him what he was doing out there. Pop I'm sure looked like a drowned rat, wet from the heavy rains. Carrying a stringer full of catfish and dip net in one hand, his minnow bucket and carbide light in his other hand and quite frustrated he looked at the policeman and said "What the hell does it look like?" The officer didn't say anything to his remark but did ask who was that in the car and what are they doing? My Pop again looked at the officer with a touch of disgust and said that we were his sons and that we were most likely sleeping. Satisfied that there was nothing shady going on, the officer finally left. Poor Pop had a rough night and a fishing trip he would never forget. The river came up so high that night we were unable to get our bank poles out and had to wait a couple of weeks for the river to go down enough to retrieve them.

I would like to share another story from the same spot as the last story but several years later.

This trip involves Pop, my brother-in-law and me. The night was a perfect summer night, warm but not too hot and quiet. The stars were out bright and filling the sky, bold and beautiful. There was no moon this night so it would have been quite dark without our carbides on. My brother-in-law said that he had a feeling we were going to have a good night and he wanted to carry the fish. Pop let him and told him he may regret having said that.

First run at 10pm we caught several nice sized flatheads and a couple of channels a bit smaller. We went on a second run around midnight catching about the same as the first run. We did have one pole really working hard and Pop had to go down after it because the hill was a bit steep and there was no room for all three of us by the pole. We helped by holding our lights down on him while he made several attempts with the dip net. One last try and the big flathead flipped so hard in the water he got unhooked. The water flew all the way up to us about fifteen feet back up the bank from where Pop was. He of course got soaked and looked back at us and said "Aint that the shits!" We knew better than to laugh but it was funny. Carrying the stringer on both trips my brother-in-law's arm was a bit sore.

At sunrise we went to get the poles out and get whatever fish we had on. We got to the pasture area where the cows cross the river to go over to another pasture on the opposite side. Pop always put a pole out at the base of a tree that bordered this crossing.

Memories

This morning, when we got to the spot we could tell that we had a nice one on. Pop got his dip net and went to get the fish when it decided to go down with one big surge. He made another attempt for it when it rolled and went down again this time pulling the pole almost out of the bank. Before he could get his hands on the bank pole the fish went straight out taking the bank pole with it. Pop said "Damn boys, we got us a good un'."

We always figured this spot was very deep. Pop took a pole one time and stuck it down in the water and never hit bottom. When we saw the pole surface out in the middle of the river Pop never hesitated, going in right after it. My brother-in-law and I just knew my dad was going to end up with a wet butt. He managed to get ahold of the pole and he hung on for dear life. That big ol' boy first led Pop down river and then turned and headed up river. Back and forth he went with Pop right behind him. After about half an hour of this, Pop finally was able to get him in our net...barely.

He got him out of the river and up to us putting him on the stringer as fast as he could. We already had several nice ones on there and ended up catching a few more. When we crossed the river to get to the other side it was all my brother-in-law could do to hold the fish up out of the water. He said that he was not about to let that big boy back in that water. When we got home we weighed all of the fish. We ended up having a total of 15 flatheads and channels with a total weight of 75 pounds. Our big one was also a flathead that weighed 13 pounds by itself. This trip was one of my more memorable ones. Over the years Pop had 3 fishing trips that he caught a total of 29 catfish, most of them being channels. He was never able through the years to get that 30th one…he sure tried though.

This will be a short memory but one that I shall never forget and my brother-in-law laughs about even to this day. We were once again down at the same spot where we caught the 13 pound flathead, this time though it was just I and my buddy who later became my younger sister's husband.

This story is not about the fishing itself, no it really is more about our use of my Pop's carbides. For those of you who do not know what a carbide light is, let me explain. This light goes back years ago and was used in many situations where the worker needed light but also needed both of his hands in order to do his job. For convenience, these lights were many times fastened to helmets the workers wore. They had a shiny reflector which would reflect the light from a flame in the center of the reflector.

Memories

The flame was the result of water making contact with carbide. Carbide is small stone like matter that will powder easily. When combined with water it creates a gas that can be ignited. This instrument called carbide light had two compartments; the upper for holding the water and the lower for holding the carbide…and the reflector was on the front. When you closed it back up and opened the lever the water dripped down into the carbide forming the gas which you then lit. The more you opened the lever the more flame you got. Now, on with the story.

We were running our bank poles about ten in the evening when we had to cross to the other side of the river. I never wore hip boots like my Dad. I was content just to wear my blue jeans and tennis shoes. Pop had always carried an extra amount of carbide with him and usually had it in his shirt pocket. I on the other hand put it in my pants pocket in a little plastic baggy. The extra was in case we ran out of light before we got back to camp, we could refresh it.

I was in the lead as we started to cross the river but unfortunately I missed the exact spot that Pop usually crossed at, I was over just a little bit too far. As I got further out into the river it got deeper, at this point approaching my waist. Yes, you guessed it. The river water made contact with the carbide in my pocket and started the chemical reaction which also gets very hot. It started burning my leg and I started yelling. My buddy had no idea what was going on, he thought maybe something had attacked me in the water. The same water he was standing in. I could not tell him what was going on because I was trying to concentrate on getting out of the water. He did the same, going back to the bank we came from.

Once out of the water I was dancing on the bank from the pain as I tried to drop my pants. The only thing I could think of was to get the carbide away from my leg. When I got my composure I was able to tell him what had happened. He of course being a good buddy stood there and laughed at me. Then he joined me on my side of the river. I found out just recently from my older brother that I was really quite lucky. If I had put the carbide in a slightly more sealed container it might have actually exploded. I guess I was happy just getting burned but I learned several lessons on that day for sure.

My introduction to the so called art of hogging or noodling, whichever term is used depending on what part of the country you're from came at a fairly early age for me. It's not that I have ever done this form of "fishing" but I know those who have tried it and/or still do it. I was probably around eight or nine when I first witnessed this being done. I thought that

Memories

they were just a bunch of people having fun going for a swim in the river. I was rod and reel fishing with my Pop and my uncle in the Middle Fork Vermilion River west of Danville, close to the Vermilion Power Plant. We had been fishing for a while when I heard the racket and realized a group had moved into the river down from us. They were making a lot of noise so I asked my father what they were doing. He watched them for a short period and then told me, "It looks like they are hogging." I asked what that was. He told me that some people will reach down into the holes or hollow logs where the fish lay with their hands. Sticking their hands into the fish's mouth, they would then pull them out. I knew at that early age that it wasn't for me.

  Later in my life Pop shared some stories about some hogging accidents he had been told about by some of his fishing buddies. As I have gotten older I have learned that there are several different forms of how this practice is performed. Some simply find the fish, locate their mouth sticking a hand in the mouth for a good grip and pulling them from their bed. Pop told me of one where they stuck their hand all the way down into the fish's stomach gripping it with their fist thus paralyzing the fish. Then they retrieve the fish while having complete control of it. Someone new wanted to try it so they let him. He managed to do as instructed bringing the fish to the surface of the water. However, once he saw the size of the big catfish he got scared and let go of the stomach pulling his arm from within. The monster cat clamped down peeling off all of the man's skin…ouch! In another story he told me the man used his foot to feel the holes in his search of his large quarry. Instead of a large catfish though, the man stuck his foot into the hole of a large turtle. The turtle grabbed the man's heel and bite it completely off. Again, this is not for me.

After I started working I had a friend at work that grew up in a family that practiced hogging on a regular basis. Their method I learned was totally different than others I knew about. They sunk fifty gallon drums into the river hoping the big cats would find them and use them for their holes. Then, they would periodically check the barrels by wading out to them. They would then sit on top of the barrel and stick leg down into the barrel using their foot to feel the bottom of the barrel for a fish. Once they had determined that there was one, they would position themselves on top of the barrel in such a way so the only exit was a hole between their legs. They placed their hands in that opening so as the big cats tried to leave the barrel they could feel the mouth and slip a hook in the corner of the mouth. The hook, fastened to a strong fish line or small rope was used to hold on to the fish while someone pulled them into the bank and out of the water. This was definitely a two man operation and I still don't think I could have ever done this…but then I have never had the desire to!

~ Chapter 7 ~

"R"

Trip Out West

My wife and I have been fortunate enough to have taken two trips out west. The first was our honeymoon in 1975...several months after we got married. The second one didn't come along until much later and involved our daughters going along with us on a family vacation. We were able to see several sites such as Mount Rushmore, our first stop. Next we stopped at Bear Country which is not far from Rushmore. There we witnessed 2 black bears having a pretty good tussle right in front of our van. Our next stop, Yellowstone, is where this little story I want to share takes place.

We had already been driving for quite some time when we were nearing one of the gates to the park...the East or South Entrance I believe. We were traveling along on a two lane highway, with woods on our left side with an occasional glimpse of a river that ran parallel to the road but was down lower than we were. A few miles out from the entrance we came upon some cars parked along the shoulder of the road, not that there was much of a shoulder to park on. As we got closer I slowed down to see if we could tell what all of the people were looking at. Apparently there was something going on in the river below.

All at once one of our daughters yelled "There are moose down in the river!" We parked and all carefully got out and went over where everyone else was standing. As we got closer we could see that there was a cow moose standing on the opposite side of this river with her young calf. You could tell for some reason she wanted to cross over to our side of this very fast flowing mountain stream. The water was moving very swiftly right here and we were all amazed that the cow moose even tried to cross at this spot.

As we gazed on the cow slowly started out into the stream, edging her way across the river like she was testing its depth as she progressed. Following very close behind her was the calf. Step by step she worked herself across the stream and the calf stayed right with her. Just about a third of the way across the water had gotten deep enough that the current swept the calf from its mother's side. We all gasped and cried out as we realized the mother was about to lose her baby calf. You could tell she was panicked as she turned and headed back out of the water.

Memories

Once she was back up on the bank of the stream, the cow started prancing back in forth along the edge of the stream following her calf. You could tell she was trying to figure out how to get that calf back out of the water to safety. Meanwhile as we all looked on the calf struggled helplessly floating down stream. Finally, the cow found just the right spot to step out into the stream below where the calf was. The calf flowed right up against the massive body of its mother and stopped, struggling trying to get its feet under it and onto something solid. The cow moose slowly side-stepped and eased her calf closer to the bank. The calf now right at the water's edge managed to stand up and worked itself back up onto the bank.

We all stood there and watched in amazement as the calf got back its composure, shook itself off and then stood by its mother wondering what had just happened. As we all looked on the mother and calf slowly worked themselves up the bank, disappearing into the dense woods lining the far side of the stream. We all started clapping and yelling shouts of joy for the sight we just witnessed…the mother moose saving her baby. This was another one of those moments in nature that few get the chance to see. We all truly felt it was God's hand at work!

We were able to see many wonderful sights that day but none more beautiful than this one. Our trip through Yellowstone was blessed later on in the afternoon, we came head on into a heavy mountain rain storm. It thundered loudly and was quite scary with all of the lightning. Unfortunately for us there was absolutely no place to pull over…no shoulders at all in the mountains.

We kept on driving just like everyone else but it was very hard to concentrate on that very narrow mountain two lane with the rain coming down so hard. All of a sudden the sun started popping out to our left as it continued to rain. We came around a curve when lo and behold there it was. Right in front of us was the most beautiful rainbow that we had ever seen. It was not up in the sky like we normally see them, no this one had a backdrop of the mountain terrain behind it. In awe of such a sight I wanted to pull over to take a picture but couldn't with the string of cars behind me. The image itself was very bright with vivid colors, a mist hung around it not taking away from it a bit, instead it only added to the beauty.

We continued to drive looking for any spot that presented the opportunity to park. The further we went the image started to fade. The fact that we were losing the chance of taking the rainbow photo of a lifetime only added to our mounting anxiety. We were coming around yet another curve in the road when all of a sudden I heard my wife shout, "There it is, a place for us to pull over." We, along with every car

Memories

behind us pulled over into that tiny little spot just long enough to take that shot. But...you guessed it. We all were disappointed at the fact that the rainbow was all but gone. We took the picture but the dynamics just weren't there. That breath taking photo opportunity was short lived and not to be had. We were disappointed but still have the memory in our minds like it was yesterday. I have seen many rainbows through the years, some very nice double rainbows. I have even gotten nice pictures of some of them. This one however will always remain one of the few unreplaceable pictures I wish I could have gotten to share with you!

~ Chapter 8 ~

"R"

<u>A Visit with Pop</u>

This chapter will be a special one for me and a very emotional one to write as well. Why, you might ask? Well, because it involves a recent experience with my father who had passed away on July 6th, 2012. It took place during this year's second shotgun season for deer – specifically on December 1st and 2nd which were on Saturday and Sunday. Some of you may have a hard time believing that this really happened and others will accept it without question.

When I came in from hunting on that Sunday evening my wife informed me that our nephew had told her he had a very strange dream while he was hunting – yes he must have fallen asleep. He told her of this particularly strange dream and later shared it with us during our Christmas get-together. For me though it wasn't really a strange dream for him to have because this was to be a very special weekend

Memories 79

indeed. At this point I decided to share with her what had happened to me, mainly because I was both excited and at the same time somewhat confused.

You see all through my growing up Pop and I got closer and closer until at one point I felt we were buddies more than father and son. He started us boys in early introducing us to his love for hunting and fishing. At a young age I spent a lot of time out in nature learning everything I could from my Pop. During the summer we spent every weekend down at the river fishing for catfish. Nobody knew that river like my Pop, nor could they catch them "cats" like he did. I was proud of him and his love for the outdoors and wanted to be just like him. During the fall and winter he taught me how to hunt squirrels, ring-necked pheasants, rabbits and white-tailed deer. As a family we grew up and survived from the meat we hunted. I loved my father very much and still do.

Also at the very early age of eleven or twelve he taught me his trade of carpet installation. I spent many years as an apprentice helping him with his moonlighting jobs – teaching me a trade and also bringing in money for the family. During my senior year of high school I worked with him as part of a work program at school. It was a bit of a problem for him though because he lost time during the early part of the day waiting on me to get on the job because what I did came first. So I decided to graduate mid-term and went to work fulltime with my Pop. This was a much better situation for him and I loved the work –

who wouldn't want to work side by side with the man he admired.

As I mentioned earlier, through the years my relationship with my Pop grew into more of a hunting buddy or fishing buddy. The father/son relationship was still there but was not a dominate part of our feelings for each other. I think it was a pride thing for him to watch us boys progress in our love for things that he loved so much. If you knew my Pop the way we did then you would have known that his hunting and fishing was always his first love to the end – just behind his love for Mom of course.

I've shared this with you only as a preface to the weekend I wish to tell you about now. This second season Saturday morning hunt started no different than any other day. I was in my little hunting blind just before daybreak, settled and ready to enjoy the day. You have to understand that for me getting a deer is not the important part of my hunt. No, on the contrary, it is secondary to my joy for watching nature unfold before me. As the daylight filled our timber the woods became filled with multitudes of squirrels chasing each other for fun and other things. You see this is the time of year that many of the animals are filled with sexual energy. Watching them chase each other is more entertaining than watching the best of shows on TV. Their play is equal to that of a couple of kittens frolicking or puppies pouncing around.

Memories

As I sat there enjoying the show a crane flew in and settled on a downed tree trunk stretching over the creek which runs through our woods. It stood there motionless observing the waters flowing below it, watching for the slightest sign of a fish or other form of aquatic life that may reside in our creek. The day before, I watched one that lit actually into the creek and walked along in the water. I saw it catch three fish before it spotted me and flew. I was attempting to take pictures of it when it spotted me move. You can't out smart natures creatures, at least not very often.

While enjoying these interactions I decided to have a cup of coffee. As I opened the thermos the aroma from the steaming brew filled my little hut. Settling back in my chair and sipping my coffee it was only a matter of a few moments when it happened. I was staring out through the openings in my hut when the image of my Pop filled my mind's eye. It was the image of him as he looked when he was around my age now. The image was clear and very vivid and I sat there viewing my Pop like I hadn't seen him for years. It was a pleasant memory for me and yet it wasn't exactly a memory. A strange feeling came over me and the image disappeared from my mind's eye as quick as it came. All of a sudden as I looked out over the timber in front of me I realized it wasn't my eyes taking in the scenery…no, not at all. I felt like Pop had taken over my body as it were, he was in fact taking part in the hunt I had started. He was sitting there in my chair and sipping from my cup of coffee.

For several minutes he sat there taking in exactly the same images I have enjoyed each and every day. Although I realized it was him, I was completely aware of everything he was seeing. It was like we had become one, what I saw he saw and vice versa what he saw I saw.

I was completely at peace with what was unfolding before me on this day. As soon as it started it ended and I was alone again. I sat there thinking about what had happened and in my own way was trying to analyze it. The same exact scenario unfolded several more times through the rest of the day…each time as before. As I called an end to my afternoon, I slowly worked my way up the steep hill and to our house. Once inside, I chatted with my wife. During this time I told her only of the critters I watched throughout the day. I did not speak of what took place with Pop, only because I wasn't sure yet why it happened.

Sunday morning came and the day was pretty much a carbon copy to Saturday. The episodes with Pop were exactly as they were on Saturday. We shared the day together, he as me and I as him. These again were just momentary acts as part of the play of the day. As I sat there in between each visit I tried to figure out just what was happening to me and a thought occurred to me. I was providing my Pop the chance for one last hunt. The last few years because of his health he has not been able to enjoy the time in the outdoors like he once had. Pop I believe had

Memories

gotten to the point that I have come to…that getting a deer is secondary to the joy of spending the time enjoying nature. As I mentioned before, we are very similar in many ways…this was one of those ways. Once again the day came to a close and my hunt was over so I worked my way up the hill for the last time this season.

Inside the house I was told by my wife of the dream shared with her by our nephew. He spoke of it as though it was a strange yet wonderful thing to happen to him. I understood it because of what took place to me during the same time. I proceeded then to tell her my adventure from this weekend. She listened intently and understood as I knew she would. I spoke of it with my sister and told her I wanted to share it with the family at our Christmas gathering. The time leading up to our Christmas was filled with much anticipation.

At Christmas I waited for the right time to share Pop's visit and the time came. As I began to speak of the events of that weekend my emotions flowed as did my tears…they usually do when my emotions run. The time went quickly and I am sure I didn't tell every little detail of the day but everyone understood. My point was to let them know that Pop was given one last opportunity to enjoy his life's love. Hope you enjoyed it, Pop!

On the way home we were discussing it and my daughter made a suggestion that I believe could be a possibility. We still have his ashes in our house. We have not technically put his spirit to rest. Maybe because of this, he is there with us and close at hand providing him the chance to share in my hunt. Don't know if that was what happened but what I do know is this…this is one weekend I shall never ever forget!

Pop is in his final resting place now and shall never be forgotten. He managed to leave me with many memories but this one will always top them all. Love you Pop, thanks!

~ Chapter 9 ~

"R"

Draw

I am reminded recently of a time these many years ago of thoughts that are not in my memory, no instead they existed in the events my Mom shared with me many years later. It was my recent friendship with Buck Taylor who played "Newly O'Brien" on TV's classic series of **"Gunsmoke"** that brought back to me these precious memories. You see when I was a youngster growing up in central Illinois, Gunsmoke was a must see in our home. We never missed an episode of it and when we went to visit my Dad's parents on a Sunday evening my grandpa would be sitting in front of the TV watching Gunsmoke…you best not disturb him. I learned, well you might go so far as to say memorized the opening shootout between Marshall Dillon and the bad man. I knew Matt's every move in precise detail.

I have told you this in an attempt to set up for you this specific moment that my Mom shared with me when I got older and could appreciate it. You see I had what was referred to as a sleepy or "lazy" eye but in my case it was simply a weak muscle that needed to be repaired. After they did the surgery on my eyes they covered both of them with a bandage so I was unable to see. I spent about a week at the hospital so they could take care of me during the healing process and during this time I stayed in what I would term as a baby bed or "crib". It had high sides on it that would roll down for them to get in where I was. Now you have to remember I was five years old in a baby bed and under normal circumstances I'm sure I could easily have climbed out of it but with my eyes covered with patches and the wrap I could see absolutely nothing...I still tried though, I'm told.

Being that age and being caged up as it were I was getting very restless. Time came for me to be taken home and Mom being the typical mother wanted to protect me from anything and everything. I loved to climb and knew where she kept certain goodies in our cabinets. She would leave the kitchen for a moment and I would start climbing up onto the cabinets to find that precious goody I was in search of. Much to my discontent Mom would show back up and of course make me get down. Now remember my eyes are covered so I can see nothing, absolutely nothing. Then there were the times I would get on the couch and stand on my head and hands with my back braced against the back of the couch. With all of this activity she was worried that I would hurt myself or do something to my eyes. Mom decided to call my doctor to see if these activities would hurt me in any way. The doctor simply told her that I should be just fine and if I should happen to hurt myself then I would stop. That was not what she wanted to hear but she accepted it as the doctor's advice and left me alone, as much as she could.

So I guess you would say I was a typical five year old full of energy and needing a release. You might also say that one of my releases was watching TV only now I was unable to do that…so I listened. I knew my shows and when they came on, even at five I was a human TV guide. Well you guessed it, one of my favorites to watch was Gunsmoke and I never missed it. The purpose for this whole reflection was to tell you of this part coming up. My Mom said the minute that I knew it was time for Gunsmoke to start I would get my little holster on with my toy six shooter. She said I would stand right in front of the TV listening and at that precise exact second that Matt pulled his gun from his holster mine was leaving my holster and we shot that bad man together. They made sure I wasn't standing to close to the TV or I might have hit the picture tube. If it hadn't been so cute she said they would have made me sit down but they all thought it was funny to watch me react to the "sounds from the TV" since I could not see a thing. It was weeks before I got the patches off of my eyes and I copied this same routine week after week until I once again could see.

I have always loved to reflect to this time and it makes me laugh to think that even at such an early age we can be programmed…you just need the right trigger to set it off. To this day whenever I watch the **"Gunsmoke"** reruns this memory comes back to me. Yes, occasionally I still "draw."

~ Chapter 10 ~

"R"

Memories of Canada

In the summer of 1972 after we graduated from high school, three of us; me and my two buddies from school headed to Canada. The destination was an old children's home. In the early part of summer while serving as counselors at a church camp we met a missionary who worked at this home. He spoke of a need they had for volunteers to do work at the home which was in need of repairs. The three of us agreed to go up as a vacation to help them out by doing what we could.

The trip up was quite adventurous in itself. It was around midnight when we all decided to stop to grab a bite to eat at a roadside restaurant in Flint, Michigan. Now feature this, three high school age boys entering a place being run by three girls all about the same age. Well, being healthy young "men" we started figuring which of them each of us wanted.

After eating, one of the girls came over to our table and asked me if I could help her with something in the back. When I stood up to go with her my two buddies looked at me and grinned because they just knew I was going to get "lucky." Once we got back there she asked me if I could open a pickle jar for her. I reached for the jar and wrapped my hands around the lid. The lid came right off with just a gentle squeeze. I handed her the lid, walked out to my buddies who were both looking at me bewildered. We paid and left. In the car they asked me what happened, I told them…strange thing was the lid wasn't even tight. They both said you idiot and explained to me why she really called me back there. You know it just didn't occur to me that was what she wanted, darn.

About 7am the next morning found us in a very rough part of Detroit needing gas, Harlem my buddies told me. Three white boys our age in that spot just wasn't making us feel very safe so we got our gas and got out of there. Funny, all three of us needed to pee but we chose - wisely, to wait until later to go.

Later that day we arrived at our destination which was Flesherton, Ontario, Canada. When we got to the children's home they wouldn't let us park the car next to the building. It seems that one of us ran over a dead skunk on the highway through the night which left the car smelling real sweet. That someone was me.

Memories

While we were at the home our appointed job was to lay underlayment down in three of the first floor rooms...large rooms. They had a church group that was coming the following week to lay linoleum tiles or asphalt tiles, I don't remember which. As long as we got that done for them then we were free to do as we wanted with the rest of our time. Two evenings we went horseback riding and one evening we went to one of the lakes to fish.

Now even though the head of the children's home was an older couple, the one who we met at our church camp was their assistant Mike Beecher, his wife's name was Diane...two of these stories are about her. One I will share now. One morning I got up, started washing up which also included shaving. Now it seems that I was the only one in this home who shaves. The head of the home wore a beard, neither of my buddies shaved and it seems that Mike also didn't have to shave. One of my buddies hollered, **"Who wants to see Bob shave?"** Well several of the young boys wanted to watch, as well as Mike's wife Diane. It seems she told someone that she thought watching a man shave was one of the sexiest things you can see. Mike knew she felt this way and heard her say she wanted to watch me. Needless to say she didn't come watch me on this occasion, thus started the friction between the two of them as well as Mike and me.

The first of our horseback rides was fairly mild with not much happening. The guides were just young kids, well younger than us. We started kidding with them telling them we were up there to avoid the draft...draft dodgers. That got them going. They had all kinds of questions for us. The second time we went was completely different. First, they gave me a horse they called the old gray mare. I found out before the end of the night this reference didn't fit my horse at all, they found it humorous though. I mounted her and then she decided to head back into the barn...with me still on her back. This may not have been a big problem except their barn was stone and the horse just barely fit through the door, so as she went through the door I had to hug her back as tight as I could. I still managed to get my back scraped on the top of the door. Sitting in the stall, still on her back I hollered, **"What do I do now?"** They laughed, told me to get off and bring her back out...which I did. We spent the next hour playing tag on horseback which was a blast. We had to be careful because it was a bit hilly, as well as there were large stones in the field. We crossed over a two lane highway into another area they have for riding. Our riding tamed down, we just rode and talked mostly in this section. Heading back to the gate where we entered we were on a dirt path. One of horses spooked and that was all it took, my old gray mare was off and running. It seems that she is a spirited horse who likes to run and it doesn't take much to get her going. I could hear them yelling to me to get her stopped but nothing I said to her was working. She was full out with no intent to stop and that gate was getting closer and closer. To this day I

Memories

don't remember what I said but I do remember that I YELLED IT. Right at the gate she came to a sudden stop with me just about being thrown over the gate. How I stayed on is a mystery to me but I'm sure I was all flustered when they caught up with me. The boys were laughing at me saying, ***"Looks like the old gray mare is still what she used to be."*** I just thought it wasn't funny. We were out so late riding that the boys needed us to help walk the horses to cool them down, which we did.

    I believe it was Friday night when Mike decided to take us out fishing. He and Diane drove us to a nearby lake which was absolutely beautiful. Mike stopped and got some bait before we got there. He had told us when we first met him at summer camp to bring our rods with us, he would make sure that we got a chance to use them. Once we got to the lake and parked, we all chose our spots to sit. The lake was fairly square and we parked near one of the corners. Mike and Diane got their stuff and headed down the right side of the lake. Both of my buddies found a spot close to the car, I walked down the left bank to the next corner and sat down…so there was a long distance between myself and Mike and Diane. We all did our own fishing until the sun was starting to go down. The next thing I knew Diane was standing beside me and we started talking. I found out later that she came by my two buddies and asked where I was. We talked for a bit until I heard Mike calling for her. She left me and went back in the direction of the corner where my buddies and the car were. About half an hour later it was getting close to dark so I stopped fishing and headed back to the car. When I got there my two buddies were standing right there where they had been fishing. I asked where Mike and Diane were and they said when Diane came back from being with me they headed to the car. They both indicated that we should not go back to the car until we were called and then asked me what happen between me and Diane. I told them that we just talked but I never thought that they totally believed me. Awhile later Mike called us to the car, and we left. That night when we went to bed we talked about it and decided that they must have made up in the car. I am sure glad that they were able to patch things up…never got into so much trouble for having done nothing.

     Our trip home was fairly uneventful except for two different episodes. One, when we were coming through the border one of my buddies said we had drugs in the trunk when we were asked by customs if we had anything to claim. I thought they were going to strip down the car and us but everything worked out okay. Next, the same buddy when we were coming through Michigan wanted to pick up a hitchhiker, cute little girl. Now get this, we are in my other buddy's Maverick. It is a small car with the three of us in it and all of our stuff…where are we supposed to put her? He wanted to dump part of our belongings out in order to make room for her. Needless to say we didn't stop

Memories

for her. That was a topic of conversation for quite a bit of time after that. With everything that happened on that trip we all still had a great time and experience outside of our country. It was beautiful up there for sure!

~ Chapter 11 ~

"R"

<u>Ice Sparkles in the Sun</u>

It was the winter of 1992, second weekend of the 92' Deer Hunting Shotgun Season. All of the members of our group who didn't get a deer the first season usually plan on going this second season trip. However, as luck would have it a major winter storm was brewing, heavy snow accumulation along with ice. My older brother was the only one in our group who really wanted to go and he managed to talk me into tagging along. The trip down seemed very long because of the weather but we managed without any incidents. I was truly amazed that we were able to drive up the steep road that takes us up into the hills because it was basically a sheet of ice but he drove right up it.

We slept in the back of his pickup inside an uninsulated topper. My kerosene heater warmed it up

Memories

at first but we were parked on a slant and half way through the night we lost most of the flame on the wick. Our heat soon transformed into condensation on the bare metal which by early morning was frozen. We woke up to the realization that we were sleeping in an icebox...I had never been so cold in my life.

We decided to go ahead and hunt mostly out of the need to build up some much needed body heat. My plan was to head down to the end of the fire trail and then cut off into the bottoms. I figured that as cold as it was the deer would be bunched up together in a group and that bottom seemed the likely spot for that. Little did I know that getting there would be so difficult. The ice coated the top of the snow and made walking very difficult...nearly impossible. As I made my way down the hillside I had to grab a tree with each step I took to keep from sliding down the hill. The ice was thick enough you couldn't even break through it. That kept you from getting a good footing which along with the slickness of the ice made it all interesting to try to navigate on.

After a long difficult walk I finally made it down into the bottom. The snow here was fairly deep and I didn't notice any signs at all that a deer was anywhere in the area. I took off walking through the vast bottom, looking for tracks and trudging through the drifts...it is no wonder the deer chose not to be there. I finally had reached the edge of the timber when I came upon a fence line which meant private property. I decided to take a breather and looked down at my watch...it was already 10:00, where had the morning gone. I had been on the move since around 5:30 and what I had eaten for breakfast was long gone. Since there weren't any signs here I decided to check out another spot which was on the way back to camp.

When I turned around to start back, that was when the scene hit me head on like a locomotive. The sun was out and even though it was very cold the sunlight was bright enough to warm your insides just to look at it. As I said the snow was drifted and fresh, virgin and untouched it made me feel as though I was in a world covered with a blanket of cotton. Even though it was very cold the icy water was flowing swiftly in the creek beds that ran along the bottoms of every ravine. The sound of the water movement played as music to my ears. The snow covered just about everything it possibly could with no exceptions. Occasionally, you would see a shower of the white released from the branches.

Standing there admiring the scene, taking this all in as a photograph etched in my memory was just not enough. The sun came out bright and bounced off the snow lighting up a multitude of sparling diamond like facets. It was as though the sun was glimmering through each individual snowflake. Everywhere I looked was an array of this sparkling wonderland, so beautiful…and yet that really doesn't describe it to you enough to do it any justice.

Memories

As my gaze turned upward into the trees I notice the ice that covered each branch. Even though the branches were weighted down under the frozen rain, that by itself is not what caught my eyes. Again, the sun danced among the laden branches reflecting through the ice like prisms. The essence of the mass of ice that dwelled within those tree branches was the evidence, the cruel remains of the harsh storm from the day before. The wind added to this show by slowly moving the branches back and forth changing the scene from one moment to the next. The backdrop of the blue sky highlighting the shadows of the forest was a sight that no description could do justice to.

I remember that scene over and over and even to this day regret not having a camera with me to capture the splendor of the moment that lay before me. It was one of those once in a lifetime sort of pictures that shall forever remain in my memories!

~ Chapter 12 ~

"R"

A Shot of Whiskey

    My mother had a thoughtful heart and looking back at it now I believe she thought she was doing the right thing…I thought she was trying to kill me. Let me explain that remark. You see back when I was a youngster in school I just loved to walk both to and from school. That lasted all the way up into my high school days. As a senior though, I drove because I went to school half the day and then worked with my Pop the remainder of the day.

    Well back either in the winter of my ninth grade or the winter of my tenth grade, I don't remember for sure which one it was, that is when this happened. You see I am a hairy person and developed that way at an early age. I was the only one in my ninth grade class with hair on my legs and chest which made it quite embarrassing during PE shower time. The guys really razzed me about all of my hair. At that same time I decided to start shaving and then it happened, I grew a mustache. That is where this story picks up.

I came in from my long walk home from school just about frozen. It was extremely cold with the wind blowing fiercely into my face. By the time I reached our house I actually had ice cycles hanging from my little mustache. I must have looked a sight, like a whipped little puppy. My mother came into the kitchen and took one look at me…that was all it took. While mom walked over to the cabinet I set my books down and then took off my coat and hat. She had poured something from a bottle and walked over to me. Now I wasn't paying any attention to what she had but I just knew that it had to be some awful tasting cough or cold medicine.

I really should have known better because she handed it to me in a shot glass but I just figured she did that for measurement. To get this over with as fast as I could I tipped my head and swallowed it all in one full gulp. My mistake! My insides felt like they were on fire and my eyes must have been bugged out of my head. You heard of the book "Fifty Shades of Grey", mom said I turned fifty shades of red…and I felt it. I truthfully thought I was dying and I yelled at her, "What did you just give me?" She was only trying to help warm me up quickly. She said, "I gave you a little shot of whiskey." Not feeling nor understanding her loving motherly gesture at that time I said, "Don't you ever do that to me again." She didn't. To this day I am not a drinker and that very well could be the reason why. I look back now and can see the humor in the moment…but not back then!

~ Chapter 13 ~

"R"

<u>Death of a Fawn</u>

      In the spring a few years back we had a terrible storm pass through. It lasted for quite some time with heavy rains, gusting strong winds and some of most active lightning and loud thunder we have ever heard or seen. It continued well into the night but come the next morning it had passed and the sun was out and bright. Now this was late enough in the spring that we already had sighted several does with little fawns. There was one of them that had a pair of little ones, this one young doe had only a single fawn with her.

      I don't remember where we were going back then but we walked out to the car to leave when I saw it. Couldn't tell for sure what it was at that distance but something was laying in our front yard. The yard was still wet from the storm the night before so I tried to be careful as I walked, my shoes got wet anyway. As I approached I could tell it was a fawn lying there, not asleep…dead.

I examined the poor thing for signs of why it died but could find no apparent signs nor was there a drop of blood anywhere. The mother was nowhere to be seen which was odd for one so young. I looked back at my wife and told her what it was. She held it in but wanted to cry. I picked up the young fawn and carried it into the woods where I laid it back down hoping the mother would find it. I placed it on the trail they used most going in and out of the woods.

After going back into the house, washing my hands and changing my shoes we left…I believe we were headed to the store to buy groceries which took a couple of hours. When we returned there was a doe standing in our front yard. She watched us pull in. We parked and unloaded the car, still with her watching us which is unusual because they normally run away as we are coming down the drive.

Once in the house, groceries put away we started watching her. She was standing basically right where the fawn had died and I realized it was the doe and she could smell her baby. She paced back and forth across the front yard looking for the fawn. With a puzzled look in her face she went back and forth most of the day, looking…not finding. Then one time when I looked out she was gone.

Memories

  The next two days were much the same with her searching the yard for the fawn but not finding it anywhere. She would return to the spot the fawn died and put her nose down to the spot. Then bringing her head back up she would start the search once more. It was just breaking our hearts to watch her torment, her frustration at not finding her baby. I realized that I messed up when I moved the fawn by picking it up. If I had left it partially on the ground and drug it then the doe could have followed the smell into the woods. I don't know why I didn't think of that then and looking back now I honestly don't know why I didn't bury it. I just wasn't thinking, shocked I believe from the fawn's death.

  To this day we have no idea why the fawn died. The storm was massive the night before. A loud clap of thunder may have frightened the young fawn into a heart attack. Lightning may have hit the poor thing although I saw no exterior signs of trauma. The wind was extremely strong with heavy gusts, it is possible the wind picked the fawn up and dropped her into our yard…the blow killing it. All of these are mere speculations and any one is a possibility, we will never know for sure. The doe finally gave up and did not return on that fourth day. One thing for certain is this…we shall never forget it!

~ Chapter 14 ~

"R"

Celebrity Connections

You always treasure the memories of meeting someone famous whether it was a planned meeting or accidental. I actually have a couple of both that I would like to share with you. I am sure in my youth I saw some local celebrities such as Sheriff Sid who was on a local TV show in Champaign, IL. However, I was young enough I just don't remember all of those.

The very first encounter with a celebrity that I do remember was Johnny Weissmuller, probably best known for his portrayal of **Tarzan – The Ape Man.** He grew up as Peter Johann Weissmuller born on June 2, 1904 and lived until January 20, 1984. At the age of nine he contracted Polio and at the advice of his doctor he swam to build up the muscles in his legs so he could walk. He got so good at swimming that he became a German/American competition swimmer.

Memories 107

Known as one of the world's fastest swimmers in the 1920's he set 67 world records and won 5 of the Gold Medals in Olympic competition. Later on, he was to become Edgar Rice Burrough's 6th Tarzan…in my opinion the best one in that role.

Back in the early 60's, Mr. Weissmuller came to do a promotion for Riley Mobile Homes on Route 45 north of Urbana. My mother took us kids to see him, all of us except my older brother. When we walked in and saw him I went speechless. I could not get out a word. I guess I was in awe of this bigger than life man I had admired for so long. He was dressed in his Jungle Jim outfit, another role he performed in the movies. Sitting on the table in front of him was the knife he used in the movies. I shook his hand and got a picture of him, Jane and Boy, autographed of course. This was my very first experience with a celebrity and I wish I had it to do over. What a thrill!

The next celebrity I was to meet came just a few years later and was unplanned. My uncle took me to the Danville Airport with him so I could watch some parachutists. He was flying the plane for them and asked me if I would like to go watch, which I did.

While we were there a plane came in unexpected with some engine trouble needing looked at. When the pilot got off the plane who should it be but none other than the well-known western actor Dale Robertson.

Now Dale Robertson was born on July 14, 1923 as Dayle Lymoine Robertson and lived until February 27, 2013. He was a very well-known western actor and had roles in many movies, most of them I believe to be westerns. One of his best known roles was on television on the program "Tales of Wells Fargo" and he was the final host of "Death Valley Days."

While Mr. Robertson's plane was being worked on my uncle walked me over to meet him. His pretense was to introduce his young nephew to the famous Hollywood Actor but looking back on it now I'm sure he wanted to meet him and used me as the excuse. I don't care because I was thrilled. Being older than I was with the previous experience with "Tarzan," I was able to hold a conversation this time and truly enjoyed talking with Dale as he asked me to call him. We had to leave shortly after our lengthy conversation so I didn't get to talk with him again but will always treasure that one and only passing with him.

Memories

Third on my list once again was unplanned but a great thrill. Each year for special events such as our birthdays or anniversary we head over to our favorite place to eat – The Beef House. Now the Beef House is no stranger to celebrities but we had never met any there...until this time. We happened to be over there in June a couple of years ago for our anniversary. We had already been seated and enjoying a salad when who should walk in and sit down at the table next to us but Mr. Jerry Van Dyke along with a group of friends and family.

Jerry Van Dyke is originally from Danville, Illinois where we live now. He was born on July 17, 1931 and of course is the younger brother to the very famous Dick Van Dyke. He started developing himself as a comedian while in high school in Danville. I'm told he and his brother Dick came by their comedy quite honestly. Their father, "Cookie" used to perform downtown drawing crowds as he told his yarns and they say he was funnier than both of his boys. I have also found out that their mother is a direct descendant from the Mayflower. Jerry has quite a varied acting career but is probably best known for his performance on "Coach" from 1989 playing until 1997.

We did not wish to embarrass him or make spectacles of ourselves so we just kept eating. As we ate, we sat there and listened to the conversation, not really wanting to eavesdrop but still the curiosity was there. There was some normal discussion, however he did share several stories with his group which we thoroughly enjoyed. After we were done and leaving our table I could not resist. I stopped, excused myself for intruding and introduced myself to Mr. Van Dyke. I told him it was truly a pleasure to sit in that room with him and his group. Then I said I just wanted to meet him and shake his hand to which he smiled at me and said, "Not a problem at all. Thank you for stopping and saying hi." He stood, shook my hand…I wished him well and we left. From their discussion I was to discover that both he and Dick came home for the funerals of two dear friends of theirs but Dick had to leave shortly after the funeral or he too would have been there with them at The Beef House. Now what a thrill that would have been to see both of them!

Last on my list but definitely I hope not the last in my life is my contact with actor and my friend Buck Taylor. I recently had contact with Buck on Facebook. We friended each other there and had several short exchanges and I was to find out quite by accident that Buck is an accomplished watercolor artist and has been for 25 plus years.

Buck was born as Walter Clarence Taylor III sharing the same name with his father and also with his grandfather. He now carries the name of "Buck"

Memories

Taylor and later became quite well known for the role he played as **Newly O'Brien** on "Gunsmoke"…a role in which he played a gunsmith and later became one of the deputies. Buck's father is the well-known "Dub" Taylor, known as a character actor and quite well known in his own right. At seventy five, Buck is very active still doing movies, actively participates in team roping in rodeos, does his paintings and is the painter of the posters for rodeos. This is actually where I was to become better acquainted with Buck.

Once I found out that Buck painted I visited his website to view his accomplished work. I fell in love with his most recent painting at that time which was known as "The Long Branch Saloon." I purchased the picture and was very excited when I received it. Just a short time after that I went in and purchased three more of his paintings; one of Matt Dillon, one of Miss Kitty, and the last being of the deputy Festus Haggen. When I tried to purchased them there was trouble with running my credit card on their end. The lady told me that someone would call me to retrieve my info once their system was working again.

I was at my folk's home getting it ready to sell and I fell asleep in my father's recliner. I was awaken by a call coming in on my cell phone. I answered it and knew who it was the minute I heard the voice…it was Buck Taylor. He actually called me himself to get the info for the purchase of his pictures. We had an incredibly pleasant conversation which lasted at least half an hour. I found Buck to be very personable and he treated me as if he had known me for years. After we hung up I was quite in awe of what just took place.

A few days later I was to see a picture Buck did of him and his dad. I had to have that picture but when I looked I couldn't find it on Buck's website. I called and asked about the picture but the young lady could not tell me anything about it. She said that she would check into it and would have someone call me back. A couple of days later once again I was at my parent's home when a call came into me...again it was Buck. We began talking and he told me that yes that was one of his paintings and that it was actually one of his most requested ones. I asked if he could add it to my most recent order if it hadn't already gone out and he said that he would take care of it. Again we had a very pleasant conversation in which I shared an exciting recent experience with my late father. Buck listened to my story and then shared a similar one of his own. After we hung up I was so taken back by the way that Buck treated me that I decided to give him a gift in appreciation. I ended up sending personalized signed copies of my first two books to him.

Later, when I received the prints I purchased I found out that Buck actually sent me a gift as well not knowing when he did so that I had sent him a gift. I found when I opened the package that Buck had sent me the picture of him and his father free of charge but also sent me his most recent rodeo poster also free of charge. One night when I got home I saw that there

Memories

was a message on our home phone and when I checked it I discovered it was a message from Buck. He called to thank me for the gift of my books…he was thrilled to get them. I just wish that I had been home to talk to him for a third time. Once my third book came out I sent him the third one so he would have the complete trilogy. I'm am thrilled to say that he is now one of my friends and plan someday to go to one of his shows to meet him personally!

~ Chapter 15 ~

"R"

The Mob: It's Who You Know

What I am about to share with you may be hard for some to believe especially if you lived in my hometown of Champaign, Illinois but it is true. This information was given to a friend and fellow author in an interview with my Uncle Henry Sansone. This is a story about his family and their connection/dealings with the mob.

Many of you may remember the old popcorn wagon that graced several of the streets in downtown Champaign from 1924 to 1974, owned at that time by the Sansone family. Originally this Cretor popcorn wagon drawn by a horse was converted to a popcorn truck in 1921 when they mounted it onto a Ford Model T pickup truck chassis. In 1940, after the Model T gave out Henry Sansone purchased a damaged 1940 Chevrolet convertible from Sullivan Chevrolet and had

Memories

the popcorn wagon moved to the new chassis where it remains today. For a short period from 1974 to 1977 it was owned and operated by Joan Macomber. In 1977 the popcorn truck was purchased by the local Champaign County Historic Preservation Committee and now resides in the Historical Museum. For safety reasons the 63 year old steam popper was replaced by an electric popping kettle made by the original Cretor Co. The popcorn truck is still utilized each year by the museum for special events.

    That having been said, let me get back to the reason for this chapter which is the connection of the Sansone family with the mob back in the 20's, 30's and 40's. The Sansone family originally immigrated to America from Sicily. They came through Ellis Island and found their way to Champaign. A family of eleven kids, each day was spent trying to bring income in to support and feed them all. The boys of the family found their own ways to make do. Michael Sansone purchased taffy making vending machines. Henry Sansone was to own and operate the popcorn wagon which was known to many of us for 5 decades. Frank, another son was to find his way to Chicago where he was to eventually become a driver for Al Capone. He was making trips several times a week to Champaign, Bloomington and Peoria hauling booze to the local taverns. Yet another brother Johnny owned and operated a whiskey package house which was located behind the old News-Gazette. Johnny and Frank's connections in Champaign made it much more lucrative for Capone to do his booze business in downstate markets such as taverns and gambling joints. Younger brother Joseph was involved with race cars and gambling. Since there were few jobs in the prohibition and depression times, these were the ways the Sansone sons found to support their family. Michael and Henry Sansone were the only two to find legal means to contribute to the family unit. I wish to speak of Henry who is my Uncle's father.

This reflection is not a memory for me other than the fact that I remember while growing up my Pop telling me that my Uncle Hank (Henry Sansone II) on several occasions had mentioned to him about the family having connections with the mob (mafia). We never knew what those were until we saw a book written by Maureen Hughes called "**The Countess and The Mob**" in which she interviewed and shares my uncles' memories. This is the connection Henry Sansone was to have with well-known members of the mob, Al Capone and George "Bugs" Moran. My cousin has confirmed these to be accurate.

Henry worked honestly and hard with his popcorn truck but found it difficult to support his own family on what he made from his sales. Now Henry was well known as an avid and accomplished hunter. Several of the local lawyers and business men called upon Henry to supply them with meat for formal meals they had with dignitaries and statesmen. Henry agreed to this and supplied ducks @ $3, pheasants @ $5 and rabbits for 50 cents each. News got out

Memories

about the fine dining Sansone could provide and word got to Capone about the fabulous hunting around Champaign. Henry was approached to set up a hunting trip for Capone and his boys. Capone was so happy with the results that he went on to hire Henry to provide future hunting trips for the group. In return, at the end of the day Capone rewarded him with a large roll of cash. These hunting trips were to go on over a four year period.

Realizing how lucrative his setting up and guiding these hunts had become Henry decided to expand his business to include Moran and his group. He never thought this was going to create a problem because he could set each group up for opposite weekends so they would never be together. Things went great until one weekend the dates got mixed up, this was because things were set up by word of mouth and one of the guys forgot what was said. Moran's group was already hunting when Capone's men showed up all in hunting gear. Nobody was recognized and hunting went on until one of Capone's men asked why Moran was there hunting also. That was it, the gunfire started and shortly after both sides retreated to their cars and left…some with buckshot in their backsides. This ended any future hunting trips to Champaign and Henry's connection with these two mobsters.

I remember my uncles' parents very well and have many fond memories both with the popcorn wagon as well as going to visit them at their home.

Even though I never had the pleasure of hunting with Mr. Sansone, I would have loved that opportunity. My father had that pleasure, having hunted both ducks and geese with Uncle Hank and his dad. He said the pair was unbeatable in their knowledge of the birds or their abilities of using the calls to bring them in.

~ My Reflections ~

As many of you know I have spent a great deal of my time in nature either fishing or hunting or simply enjoying the beautiful things God has created. I know many of my friends have their special little places they like to go to meditate. There are places I have been that if I lived close to them now I know they would be special places for me.

Once when my Pop and I were down checking out a place in the Wildcat Hills in Gallatin County not far from the little town of Equality, Illinois – I found such a place. We walked back as far as the road would take us. There was a man-made pond at the end. Pop dropped off on one side and started exploring and I did the same on the other side. I found myself on the side of a very long hillside. I would bet that from top to bottom it had to be a 400 to 500 foot drop and it looked to be all trees…a medium growth timber, not tall trees at all. A short way down the hill I stopped and just sat down…listened to the gentle breeze flowing through the leaves on the trees. Even though it was quite chilly out that afternoon sun just warmed my insides. It covered me in such a blanket of unbelievable peace and tranquility that I could have stayed there forever. As I looked up at the leaves I realized that I was sitting on a hillside of solid oaks, not sure what kind they were but I knew they were all the same. Wow, I was both amazed and shocked at the same time. To this day I have never found another spot like it, especially not that peaceful.

One other area gave me a similar feeling and it happened to be in that same county, just at the other end of the county. Now I'm sure that there are similar types of spots all through the Shawnee Forest, these just happen to be two I have found. The second spot was sitting on a rock bluff, also warm and peaceful. I have been in that particular spot on several occasions finding it a bit easier to get to than the first one.

Every time I have sat in this spot I have noticed little tiny lizards scurrying across the rocks. They are not only fun to watch but they can take your mind to places elsewhere. I would even go so far as to bet if you came here with troubles on your mind you could leave at least with them momentarily lost. I have spent several hours in this spot just relaxing, taking it easy, meditating…we all refer to it in different ways. I would recommend to anyone that if you can find a spot like this hang on to it. God, I think provides these places of meditation for a reason…if we used them more often maybe we wouldn't need all the drugs or medications we use for "physical ailments."

Memories

I hope by reading this you have been able to find at least one of these chapters that has touched you in some way, or better yet maybe moved you in such a way to reflect on your own real experiences. I have enjoyed this time with you and sharing some of our **"memories."**

Bibliography

Lloyd Eugene Garner; author's uncle by marriage who shared with author though general conversation.

Lowell Dean Garner; author's father-in-law who shared with the author through interview.

Maureen Hughes; author of the book called "*The Countess and The Mob*" from which I shared. She interviewed my Uncle Henry Sansone about the Sansone family.

Donna Mast; author's sister who shared tapes she made of conversations with our father – Donald Harvey Wilson

Lisa Pierce; graphic artist who designed both the front and back covers. Photos used were taken by the author and/or his family.

Donald Harvey Wilson; author's father who not only shared some of his experiences with the author but helped the author live some of his own.

Juanita Jeanne Wilson; author's mother who kept records that helped establish the times, dates, places, etc. for some of the information shared.

Front cover; photo of author's grandfather.

Author's picture; back cover – family picture taken of author around the age of 4 or 5.

CPSIA information can be obtained
at www.ICGtesting.com
Printed in the USA
FSHW022313301019
63580FS